The PILGRIM ROAD

Reflections on the Songs of Ascent in the Psalms for Lent and Easter

William G. Carter

CSS Publishing Company, Inc.
Lima, Ohio

THE PILGRIM ROAD

FIRST EDITION
Copyright © 2020
by CSS Publishing Co., Inc.

Library of Congress Cataloging-in-Publication Data: 2020946956

For more information about CSS Publishing Company resources, visit our website at www.csspub.com, email us at csr@csspub.com, or call (800) 241-4056.

e-book:
ISBN-13: 978-0-7880-2959-2
ISBN-10: 0-7880-2959-2

ISBN-13: 978-0-7880-2958-5
ISBN-10: 0-7880-2958-4   DIGITALLY PRINTED

Table Of Contents

Introduction

A high school English teacher once assigned a few chapters of Geoffrey Chaucer's *The Canterbury Tales* to our class. We groaned. The ancient dialect was obtuse and we were too dull to catch the good humor of Chaucer's work. More to the point, we were never told what the work purports to be: a collection of stories from the pilgrim road, as a whole company of the faithful moves toward the cathedral of God.

The road is a great metaphor for the spiritual life. Others have traveled before us and have wisdom to share. We learn from what they have encountered along the same or similar routes. Their well-worn maps still provide the essential guidance we need. These astute travelers on the holy way share their scouting reports to us, and blessed are those who pay attention to what they hear.

In the center of the Bible, there are fifteen short songs of guidance tucked away in a larger collection of liturgical poems. These are a group of psalms, generally numbered 120-134,[1] with each one bearing the identical heading: "A Song of Ascents." The word "ascent" has a double meaning. Jerusalem was the location of the Jewish temple. It was built on the high ground of Mount Zion. Pilgrims literally climbed uphill to worship. As they did, they also moved up higher toward God.

The scholars suggest these fifteen psalms were sung and prayed by ancient Jews as they traveled toward the temple that they regarded as the house of God. It was a repeated trip, as the faithful returned again and again to Jerusalem for annual festivals, major life events, seasons of thanksgiving, and genuine occasions of prayer regarding life's circumstances.

1 Due to a slightly different numbering scheme in Latin and Hebrew, in some translations these Psalms are numbered 119-133.

The Pilgrim Road

Each recurring journey was set within the larger trek of faith. In the spiritual life, we walk the same steps repeatedly, in the hope that our souls will be deepened with each passing repetition. There is no assurance this will happen, of course. While we notice more of the passing landscape, we might also be bored by the familiarity. At any moment, we might lose our concentration or be distracted by daydreaming. The regular commuter may encounter more potential hazards than the first-time explorer.

Think of how it is when we drive down the highway. There are potholes, detours, and the unexpected hazards. A broken chunk of truck tire may suddenly appear on the pavement, requiring a quick serpentine move to protect ourselves and our passengers. In the land where I dwell, the late-night traveler must flick the headlights to ensure that no deer have wandered onto the road. And who can predict the oversized trailer that suddenly sways into our path without warning or directional signals? Sometimes the best choice is to hit the brakes, give the potential danger plenty of room, and zip by when the way is clear.

The careful traveler looks for guidance along the way. The woman with the orange flag motions when we need to slow down. A construction site posts road signs to announce fines if we put the workers at risk. The occasional flashing sign reveals our speed. Even if it looks like the road is open, cruise control can entice the most cautious motorist into a dangerous stupor. We must travel with our eyes open and our hearts awake.

I am one who has been so blessed. My first encounter with this collection of *Songs* came from Eugene Peterson, an insightful pastor and writer whose wisdom has guided me for my whole adult life. Eugene wrote a great book called *A Long Obedience in the Same Direction*,[2] once describing it to me as "a collection of

2 Eugene Peterson, A Long Obedience in the Same Direction (Downers Grove, IL: InterVarsity Press, 1978).

Introduction

well-edited sermons on a dog-eared hymnal." Since discovering that book as a college freshman, I have worn out two copies of it, thumbing through it for spiritual sustenance and never going hungry.

Many years later, it is my hope to pass along similar wisdom mined from these fifteen psalms. In three decades of pastoral work, God's Spirit has continued to instruct me, in order that I may share what I have learned with others. The lessons have come from inside and outside of life in the church. Some of these lessons, frankly, might curl your hair. Others will provide the assurance of a friendly voice that confirms what you already know. All I would ask of you, fellow traveler, is that you share similar guidance to those who journey with you. The spiritual life is too precious for any of us to travel it alone.

While I take all responsibility for the yarns that I spin in this book, I give thanks to God for the great company that surrounds my spiritual journey: for my wife Jamie, who makes her love tangible; for our children Josh, Katie, Lauren, and Meg, who give us hope for God's next generation; for our church families in Clarks Summit and Blakely that sustain us in prayer and generosity; and to an enormous gathering of friends and family that make our shared pilgrimage a daily joy.

My deepest gratitude is for my parents Glenn and Elizabeth Ann, who taught me the psalms by raising me in the Christian faith. Dad took me to the awesome mountains and taught me to look beyond them for help (Psalm 121:1-2), and Mom calmed me when I was a weaned child (Psalm 131:2). Their house has been built by God (Psalm 127:1). I dedicate this book to them.

The poet T. S. Eliot wrote, "Our end is in our beginning." I invite you to believe that. Our journey has its destination in its beginning. We travel toward the God who made us, never far

The Pilgrim Road

from the Christ who travels unseen by our side, guided by the Spirit who shines light on our path.

See you along the way!

Holy Discomfort

A Song Of Ascents

In my distress I cry to the LORD, that he may answer me:
"Deliver me, O LORD, from lying lips, from a deceitful tongue."
What shall be given to you? And what more shall be done to you,
you deceitful tongue?
A warrior's sharp arrows, with glowing coals of the broom tree!
Woe is me, that I am an alien in Meshech, that I must live among
the tents of Kedar.
Too long have I had my dwelling among those who hate peace.
I am for peace; but when I speak, they are for war.

(Psalm 120: 1-7)

When I was younger, there was something about a long car ride that upset my stomach. The discomfort was not obvious right away, but within fifty miles or so, my gut was churning. The eruption would come suddenly, and sometimes I was able to offer a last-minute warning. Everybody in the car lurched for a large coffee can and pushed it in front of my mouth. Afterward, my mom was the only one in the car to offer a word of comfort as she dabbed my mouth with a wet washcloth that she kept in a plastic sandwich bag for such occasions.

This ritual went on for a dozen years and prompted many attempts for a remedy. My parents tried motion sickness pills, told me to breathe into a paper bag, and rolled down the windows for a dash of fresh air. Nothing worked. If the cause could be identified, every attempt would be made to eliminate it. My mother read in *Good Housekeeping* that carsickness is provoked by reading a book while traveling, so she banned my novels, biographies, and magazines. I distinctly remember the sweet

9

smell of coffee poured from a Thermos in the front seat and the odor set me off. It was decreed: no more coffee.

Another time I was sitting up front with my father and everybody else was asleep in the back of the station wagon. The coast was clear, so he lit a cherry cigar to help him stay awake — and then devilishly asked if I wanted a puff. A minute later, he regretted it and my mother declared there would be no more cigars.

I cannot say why I became sick to my stomach or why one day I was no longer besieged. Maybe my stomach grew stronger with age. Perhaps a loose wire in my brain was tightened down over time. But this childhood nausea comes to mind as I reflect on the first of the pilgrims' psalms. Psalm 120 is the song of a distressed traveler. There is something deeply disturbing at the beginning of that person's journey. "In my distress, I cry to the Lord, that he may answer me: Deliver me, Lord…"

Deliver me: what an appropriate phrase! Not merely "help me" or "assist me," but *deliver* me. Carry me over the miles and take me where I need to go. It is a vague sentiment with no named destination. The travelers do not yet know where they are going. What is clear is that they cannot stay where they are. Something is making them sick to their stomachs and they need to go somewhere else.

As we begin our travels on the pilgrim road, we begin by naming whatever discomfort we feel — whether or not we understand its source. For some, there is a clash between the values they affirm and the realities they now face. The commonly assumed rules seemed clear for a while, but now something does not fit. If we played it safe or went along in the same direction with those around us, the situation has now changed.

Perhaps we accommodated ourselves to the words and motions around us, admitting quietly, "That's the way the world works." But now, we have lost our comfort with the old ways. The psalmist senses this dissonance and laments the warlike tendencies of those around him. 'They hate peace,' he says. 'I am for peace; but when I speak, they are for war.' Perhaps this is a holy discomfort, stirred up by the Spirit of God. Who can say?

I do know that there is often a discrepancy between what we hope for and what we receive. We anticipate something and do not get what we want. The results can be jarring.

I will never forget the night when my father and I took a trip to the Holy Land and found ourselves sitting by the Sea of Galilee. Our tour base was a resort town on the western shore called Tiberias. It has been around since the time of Jesus, but the city is never directly named in the New Testament. Strange, actually, since it is so old and so close to everything that Christian pilgrims want to see.

Earlier that day, we toured the ruins of Capernaum where Jesus lived, walked among the lilies where Jesus gave the Sermon on the Mount, and broke bread where Jesus fed the multitude. To top it off, we rode a fishing boat across the glass-like sea toward our hotel. It was a wonderful spring day. We decided to wander down to the shore where we could watch the sunset over a glass of wine and reflect upon the day.

Just as we settled in for a second sip, our reverie was interrupted by pounding drums and screaming guitars. There was raucous laughter and what sounded like a hundred slot machines. It was obnoxious. Then we saw it — a party boat emerging from a cove, disco lights throbbing, music churning, all of it a most unwelcome spectacle on the Sea of Galilee. We had so many uplifting experiences from the day, but the whole thing was cheapened by crass commercialism. It began to dawn on me why the town of Tiberias was never mentioned in the New Testament.

The Pilgrim Road

We wanted something holy — we had every reason to expect it — but that was not what we received.

Call it holy discomfort. A deeper spiritual life begins with the acute feeling that life around you is not as it is supposed to be. It is tainted somehow. The party boat should not have surprised me. If the truth be told, all throughout the day we had encountered gift shops and sleazy tourist traps around every holy monument. The world wants us to reduce our spiritual sites to kiosks in the shopping mall. Pay a quick visit, buy a plastic trinket, and move on.

Yet I found my soul wanting more. It struck me that such dissatisfaction may be a gift from God.

"Deliver me, O Lord, from lying lips, from a deceitful tongue." This is the singular prayer of Psalm 120. The journey toward God begins by noticing all of the deceptions, the lies, the spins, and the distortions of truth. The advertisers lie when they say a bar of soap will improve our love life. The airlines lie when they say the flight delay will not make us late. The real estate agents lie when they claim the fixer-upper will not need much work. The politicians lie when they claim they are only looking out for the rest of us. Preachers lie if they tell us the gospel will make us comfortable all the time.

Every day we have to wade through waves of deceit. Sometimes it is so subtle that it sneaks by. The newscaster may read the cue cards without knowing the news is slanted. Those who swallow such news as is may end up with their hearts poisoned.

Or maybe we have had my experience of ordering food in a restaurant and wondering why it never looks like the picture on the menu.

Sometimes the deceit is blatant and rubbed in our faces. A man told me about buying a car in northern Virginia. As he prepared to settle the bill, he learned that hundreds of dollars of fees and extra charges were sneaked onto his bill. "Are any of these required?" he asked.

"No," said the clerk, "but I am required to add them to your bill."

"Then I am requiring you to remove them," said the frustrated customer.

Some lies are so pervasive that people accept them without question. Their lives have been shaped by mistruths that have been freely passed along. Really big lies go like this: that we are in charge of our own lives — or that we are in control. It is a surreptitious little deception and can pervade everything we think or do. It can also twist our heads in the wrong direction.

Say, for instance, the elderly lady across the street cannot keep up with her dandelions and her lawn turns bright yellow. She seems to grow more dandelions than blades of grass. You should hear the neighbors complain about it. They creep over after dark and put weed killer on her lawn so that the dandelions will not invade their yards.

Can we see this for what it is? It is not compassion. The neighbors are not helping out the lady. No, they are not giving her a hand. They want to take charge and keep those pesky weeds out of their grass. Whether they realize it or not, the whole situation sets up an illusion of control. Get rid of her dandelions and make it look like a good deed. Beneath it all, the assumption seems to be that if people can get rid of the weeds, they will have a perfect lawn. And if they have a perfect lawn, they presume they will have a perfect life.

Control is one of the greatest lies of the world, because none of us can ever control very much. We cannot control the rain, the snow, the sunshine, or the wind. We cannot control our kids, or else they may grow up to resent us. We cannot control our illnesses, but merely find expensive ways to endure them.

The Pilgrim Road

I went to see my doctor, complaining of a head cold. He had a cold too, and that did not inspire my confidence. I whined for medication. He said, "Here are your choices. You can take an antibiotic for seven days. Or you can do nothing, wait a week, and the cold will be gone."

I asked, "What am I paying you for?" I was paying for the truth, of course. We will do anything to avoid the truth. Especially the truth about ourselves!

A number of years ago, my congregation sent a team of people on a mission trip to Haiti. It was a privilege to join them on the trip. We spent time volunteering in a pediatric AIDS clinic, touring a mission hospital, and visiting a literacy center developed by church people. We lived simply among peasants and that experience enlarged our world. The diet was seven nights of red beans and rice with one special feast of roasted goat. Our hosts probably spent a month's wages on the entree.

It was a good experience, but I was ready to return home. After landing in Kennedy Airport, we began the van ride back to our town. From the back seat I spoke up, "I'm hungry. Could we stop and get something to eat?" Our driver pulled into a fast food place and I ordered two of the largest double hamburgers on the menu.

Halfway through the second sandwich, the awareness of my self-indulgence slapped me awake. What was I doing? Did I think I could purge a week of sacrificial, eye-opening service by gobbling down a couple of burgers? Suddenly, once again, there was a foul feeling in my stomach.

The truth will slap us awake. When it does, we can feel like we have been hovering in the wrong place. The singer of Psalm 120 confessed of feeling like an outsider: *"Woe is me, that I am an alien in Meshech, that I must live among the tents of Kedar."* Meshech was a far-off land, hundreds of miles away, near Russia. Kedar was a tribe of wandering shepherds with a nasty reputation, the equivalent of an ancient street gang.

In other words, "I feel like I am far from home, hanging around with all the wrong people."

This is how the spiritual journey begins: with the deep discomfort of being a long, long way from home. We discover nothing fits together as it once did, so a new journey must begin. Somehow God grabs our shoulders and shakes us. We begin to pay attention to the situations we have taken for granted. We notice what we had previously ignored. Faith is on the move. Our stomachs may churn until we name the deeper hunger, until we affirm that what we are really seeking is God.

My friend Paul is a serial job hunter. No sooner does he get a new job than he starts looking over the fence for the next job. He is never content. He never puts down roots or makes long-term friends. If he has a dream, it is that the grass really *will* be greener in the next pasture. He never stops to see that grass is only grass. All it ever will be is grass. As the Bible says, "The grass withers, the flower fades, but the word of the Lord stands forever." (Isaiah 40:8)

My friend hopes for the next job. There are people who hope for the next relationship.

Others seek the next great bargain, the truly restorative vacation, or the satisfying business deal. So many of our great human hopes are substitutes for the one thing that we really want. We rush to fill the spiritual void and then discover our substitutes cannot carry the freight. Buy a new house and it has a broken back door. Make new friends and discover they gossip as much as the old friends. Buy some toys in the electronic super store and get home to discover they do not fill those hungry spaces in our souls, and the batteries aren't included. Book a vacation at the hotel pictured on the brochure and it never looks as good as it did in print.

What about the chronic church shopper? She wants a livelier worship service, a better program for her kids, or a pastor with a better haircut. All of this sounds promising until she discovers the new church has just as many sinners as the last church did. Any church that promises to meet every unchecked, unexamined "need" is guilty of false advertising. It is a great way to avoid perpetual disappointment. We can want all we want until we discover the things of this world are lousy substitutes for God. It is a lie to think we can consume God like one more consumer product. But if we pay attention to this hunger, it can drive us to start looking for the real deal.

This is how the true spiritual journey begins. Certainly we have our deep human hopes, but they must always be provisional. We wake up hungry for something the world cannot provide. That hunger — that desire for something substantial beyond what we have — that is the gift of holy discomfort, driving us forward toward God.

If you are feeling any such emotion today, take it as a gift from God. If you are feeling discontent about some situation or person in your life, see it as a holy clue to recognize that nothing on earth will completely satisfy us. No job, no hot meal, no relationship, no group of people will ever satisfy us.

We are destined to be dissatisfied until we find ourselves completely in the presence of God. This is the journey that the Psalms of Ascent begin to narrate.

God will burn away every vain dream, puncture every false hope, and correct every lie with the truth — until the day when, beyond all the counterfeits, we see the one who is our destination.

Reflection Questions

"Holy Discomfort," Psalm 120

— Where am I most dissatisfied with my life?

— What are the distortions and mistruths that I swallow each day?

— How does a consumer world make false promises about meeting my needs?

— What are the annoyances and disruptions that are driving me toward God?

— Do I want a God who meets my deepest needs, or a God who redefines them?

— Will God truly satisfy me? How?

Keeping And Being Kept

A Song Of Ascents

I lift up my eyes to the hills — from where will my help come?
My help comes from the LORD, who made heaven and earth.
He will not let your foot be moved; he who keeps you will not
slumber.
He who keeps Israel will neither slumber nor sleep.
The LORD is your keeper; the LORD is your shade at your right
hand.
The sun shall not strike you by day, nor the moon by night.
The LORD will keep you from all evil; he will keep your life.
The LORD will keep your going out and your coming in from this
time on and forevermore.   (Psalm 121: 1-8)

It is awkward to admit this, but my wife and I cannot agree on
the best place to take a vacation. If we spend a week at the beach,
I did not make the plans. I am a mountain guy. There are beach
people and mountain people. Beach people smell of coconut oil
and wear bright colors. Mountain people spritz themselves with
bug spray, put on sturdy shoes, and dress far more modestly.

You can keep the beach. I love the mountains. I would give
anything for a trip to the Canadian Rockies. In the heights, the
higher you climb, the purer the air. The view from a mountain
summit offers perspective on the little bitty troubles we have at
lower altitudes. The mountains are big and impressive, and they
have been around a lot longer than the rest of us. Mountains
demand our respect. They were around a long time before we
ever appeared. They have heard it all, seen it all, and will remain
standing for a long time after we are gone. We must negotiate
the mountains on their own terms. They will not move out of our
way.

Keeping And Being Kept

Psalm 121 looks to the mountains. That is how the psalm first catches our attention. We see the opening words on colorful calendars, beneath a photograph of Pike's Peak in its purple majesty. The first verse of the psalm appears on postcards from Montana and Mount Hood. Even the Mother Superior in the last few lines of "The Sound of Music" quotes verse one as she nods toward the Swiss Alps to suggest an escape route for the Von Trapp family singers: "*I lift up mine eyes unto the hills; from whence cometh my help?*"

This is one of the four or five psalms that many Christians recognize immediately. Faithful people have sung it for three thousand years. Like Psalm 23, it is simple and straightforward and we do not have to translate any words.

Yet while this is a favorite psalm, it is also a prayer for the beginning of a journey, the second of the songs of ascent. If the first song, Psalm 120, names our dislocation and a hunger to move closer to God, this psalm declares blessing for that journey.

Picture an old priest lifting hands to bless the departing pilgrims. The words are familiar and true: "You will travel through mountains. They will be impressive, but dangerous. When you look to the hills, remember that they will not give you any help." The big hills are beautiful, blue, and awesome — but they are also deadly quiet. If you fall into trouble, they will simply stand there and watch. If you cry out for help, the mountains will mock you with an echo.

It is natural to look to the hills because they are a lot bigger than we are. They remind us of our smallness. The mountains stand passively, insisting that we climb on their terms or take extra time to pass around them. They will not do anything to assist us. Danger can strike the traveler at any time. Beach people may slather on suntan lotion, knowing the sun could smite them by day. Mountain people pray that God will not let their feet slip.

The Pilgrim Road

A broken leg is big trouble on an alpine trail. There is no telling when trouble will confront us along the way. Threats are a given on every journey.

The ancient poet who composed Psalm 121 knew of three possible dangers for travelers. First, in the middle of the day the sun can strike, signifying that there are natural elements that can weaken or inflict pain. Danger could come from intense heat, or bracing cold winds for that matter. The world may be a beautiful place, but sometimes it is our adversary.

Second, on other occasions, people can be afflicted by emotional or mental forces beyond their control. The psalmist remembers how travelers can lose their way in the wilderness and become "moonstruck." In the ancient world, there seemed to be few explanations for the demons that disturb the human mind, except that "it must be the moon." There are forces out there that threaten to craze us.

Third, we are simply not physically strong enough to be risk-free. Loose gravel might twist our ankles. A slippery path could cause us to trip and fall. A truck may suddenly appear in our blind spots. There might be an obstruction in the road. Due to the laws of physics, we might not be able to brake or swerve in time, and even if we do, that could cause further damage. The same three dangers are with us: *Sun struck, moon struck, and slippery paths.*

A few years ago, I was driving a rented car across the Mojave Desert and got a flat tire. Apparently, our rear right tire was sun struck and the hot pavement made it explode. We were driving just west of the Nevada-California border. The last-stop casino in Nevada was within sight, about five miles away, but it was 104 degrees in the middle of the afternoon. Asking my four companions to walk with me in that heat was not my first option. There was a highway patrol call box nearby with a friendly dispatcher at the other end. Soon a mechanic appeared to help us find and change a well-hidden spare tire.

This was a Friday afternoon on the main highway between Las Vegas and Los Angeles. We were not alone for the next 110 miles to Barstow. As we wobbled along on a donut spare at 45 miles per hour, the truckers exploded past us doing 85 or more. If one of those semis had veered a little bit closer than they already had been, it would have caused more than our feet to slip. At moments, this stirred up some considerable stress inside the minivan. In time, it had the opposite effect: every time a truck blasted by, the van would shake, and all we could do was trust God and keep moving.

Sun struck, moon struck, and slippery paths — every traveler comes up against these dangers. The psalm promises that God is stronger than every one of them. That does not mean that God regularly breaks the rules of physics to protect us. If we are pushing it on a hot highway, one of our tires might blow. This is not God's fault.

But have you noticed? There are many accidents that might have turned out a lot worse than they did. There are a lot of treacherous situations from which we were quietly protected. Sometimes we discover there are "dangers, toils, and snares" from which we are secretly sheltered. The theological word for this experience is "providence." It means God provides for our care. This is the spiritual promise for our life's journey, to say nothing of our shorter side trips. We cannot always see God's protection in advance. We cannot always discern it in the whirlwind of danger, but it becomes crystal-clear after a threat has passed. And then we know in our bones that it could have been a lot worse.

When a college student named Jason was returning home during a school break, he found himself boxed in by three large trucks. Each was moving down the highway at a good clip, and

The Pilgrim Road

Jason was able to keep up in his compact car. Suddenly he noticed that the truck to his left was starting to veer toward him. Unsure if the driver could see him and having nowhere to go, he blurted out a prayer and hoped for the best.

The truck clipped his front bumper, sending him into a tailspin. As he spun twice in his lane, each time staring down the second truck that was behind him, he was sure that this was the end. He went off the road in the only place within that stretch where there were no guardrails. The truckers kept blasting along, leaving him in a crushed car and miraculously unscathed.

"This could have been a lot worse," declared the state police officer who came to his aid. When Jason's mother arrived a few hours later to give him a ride, she nearly passed out when she saw what was left of his vehicle. He had been protected and spared. A good bit of their ride home to safety was spent in awe-filled reverence and gratitude.

In the time when travelers first sang Psalm 121, many people believed there were divine beings up in the hills. These were the spirits of Ba'al, deities of a folk religion surrounding Jewish faith. Much of Ba'al worship was self-centered. There was a spirit of rain, and you gave him an offering if your crops were dry. The spirit of fertility accepted cash bribes if your cradle was empty. Ba'al religion was the pursuit of human success and pleasure. People made lavish offerings to get the gods of Ba'al in their corner. This was harder than we might think; the gods of pleasure were given to a lot of drinking and carousing, which explained why they were not very attentive. They often fell asleep with hangovers, up in the hills.

But the psalmist declares the God of Israel "does not sleep" — do you hear the difference? This is the God who watches over the whole created order. The God of Israel does not always give us what we want, but Yahweh makes covenants and sticks to them.

Keeping And Being Kept

As Martin Luther wrote in a sermon on this psalm, the hardships of life might cause us to think God has forgotten about us. When we feel this way, he said, "We should remain steadfast in faith and await God's help and protection. Because even though it appears that God is sleeping or snoring… this is certainly not so, despite the way we feel and think. He is surely awake and watching over us… Eventually we will learn that — if we can only hold fast."[3]

Six times in the psalm, like a steady drumbeat, Yahweh is described as "the keeper":

- He who *keeps* you will not slumber…

- He who *keeps* Israel will neither slumber nor sleep…

- Yahweh is your *keeper* and your shade…

- Yahweh will *keep* you from all evil…

- Yahweh will *keep* your life…

- Yahweh will *keep* your going out and your coming in, now and forever…

Nowhere does it say we will be exempt from road hazards, whether we are on a pilgrimage, a return trip from college, or a quick outing to the grocery store. None of us is "danger proof." Life's troubles are real. Like the Pennsylvania potholes around my home, they can come out of nowhere to bite us.

But the clear promise is that, in whatever comes, we will be kept. The God who loves us will not loosen his grip on us. Yahweh will keep us from evil. The God who claims us in Jesus Christ will never let us go. Are there irrational forces of destruction in the

3 Quoted by James Limburg in "The Autumn Leaves: Pages from the Psalter for Late Pentecost," *Word & World* December 3 (1992). Website: http://www.luthersem.edu/word&world/Archives/12-3_Music/12-3_Limburg.pdf

world? Yes — but they will not — and they cannot — ultimately win. We belong to God. God's keeping comes before everything else, and in the end, it is all that really matters.

After the preacher William Sloan Coffin Jr. buried his son, he stood in his pulpit ten days later and declared that no Christian, not even a preacher, is ever exempt from difficulties. One of those difficulties came as he dealt with a few religious people, clergy included, he said,

> *"...who were using comforting words of scripture for self-protection, to pretty up a situation whose bleakness they simply couldn't face. But like God himself, scripture is not around for anyone's protection, just for everyone's unending support. And that's what hundreds of you understood so beautifully. You gave me what God gives all of us — **minimum protection, maximum support**. I swear to you, I wouldn't be standing here were I not upheld."*[4]

That is a description worth pondering: God may give "minimum protection" but offers "maximum support." There are plenty of hazards on the road, but God keeps us. Nothing in life or death shall block God's possessive love for us. No doubt, there may be dangers prowling just out of sight, but the word "providence" means that the God whom we travel toward is the God who guards our journey. In many ways, seen and unseen, God watches over us.

A couple of weeks after my high school graduation, I drove my parent's Dodge into a big old oak tree. I did not mean to do it, but some friends and I were fooling around. I was behind the wheel. One of my buddies accidentally lit a firecracker inside the car and it went off. Next thing I knew, I looked back from that distraction and there was that tree, ready to greet us.

4 William Sloane Coffin, Jr., "Alex's Death", PBS http://www.pbs.org/now/printable /transcript_eulogy_print.html.

Keeping And Being Kept

This is not something I would recommend, even if you do not like your parents' car. It meant three nights in the hospital and a row of stitches in my tongue. And I ached all over for another month.

One night, as I tossed and turned in my hospital bed, I suddenly had the feeling that somebody had come in the room and was sitting on the end of my bed. I awoke with a start, reached for the lights. There was nobody there. It was unnerving. I rolled over, started to drift off to sleep.

Once again I knew somebody was there — and I mean *somebody*. It was like a possessive Mama Bear was guarding one of her cubs in the dark. I did not dare to look; I was a bit frightened by the feeling, and even more scared that she might leave. In the confidence God was fiercely present with me, I could fall back to sleep.

When morning came, my first visitor was the minister from my church. I told him about the strange experience that I had the night before. He listened for a while and did not seem the least bit surprised. Then with a sly smile, he said, "It makes sense to me. Do you remember the verse? 'He who keeps you does not slumber or sleep'."

It never occurred to me, with my wounded tongue, that one day I would tell anybody about this. But there it is. To this day, here is what I know to be true: even when it looks like there is minimum protection in our lives, God provides maximum support. As we move toward Yahweh, our God will *keep* us.

Indeed, said the psalmist, this is the essence of the good news: "God will keep your going out and your coming in, from this time forth and forever more."

Reflection Questions

"Keeping And Being Kept," Psalm 121

— Can I name some of the impediments that threaten my spiritual journey?

— Are there physical limitations, emotional disruptions, or slippery distractions that keep me from God?

— How have I experienced the physical protection of God?

— When was the last time that it felt like God had forgotten me?

— Did I snap out of it? How?

— If I am still feeling forgotten, can I name some ways that God has secretly provided for me today?

— If it is true that God offers "minimum protection," especially from our self-inflicted difficulties, how does God still offer "maximum support"?

A Glimpse Of The Destination
A Song Of Ascents — Of David

*I was glad when they said to me, "Let us go to the house of the
LORD!"*
Our feet are standing within your gates, O Jerusalem.
Jerusalem — built as a city that is bound firmly together.
*To it the tribes go up, the tribes of the LORD, as was decreed for
Israel, to give thanks to the name of the LORD.*
*For there the thrones for judgment were set up, the thrones of the
house of David.*
Pray for the peace of Jerusalem: "May they prosper who love you.
Peace be within your walls, and security within your towers."
*For the sake of my relatives and friends I will say, "Peace be within
you."*
*For the sake of the house of the LORD our God, I will seek your
good.*   (Psalm 122: 1-9)

In the first congregation where I served as a pastor, there was
the memory of a minister named Simmons. He did not serve there
for very long, for he was different from the congregation's long
string of pastors. Unlike the young pups that the church hired
right out of seminary, Simmons was near the end of his career.
He had been around the block a few times and was less tolerant
of the pettiness that would frequently surface in a congregation.
That did not endear him to many. After one ornery country
doctor got out of his pew during a sermon and shook his fist at
the pastor, Simmons had a heart attack and decided to retire.

His more enduring legacy was a piece of artwork that he
designed during his tenure. It was a simple geometric cross with
a Star of David at the intersection. This, Simmons explained, was

meant to symbolize that Christianity has Jewish faith at its center. What is most profoundly true for the Jew is what the Christian believes.

His point is well taken. Over two-thirds of the Christian Bible is Jewish scripture. A Christian cannot fully understand key concepts of sin, salvation, and shalom without a Jewish background. The Savior Jesus was a Jew. He was circumcised into the covenant, kept the commandments, celebrated the festivals, and prayed the prayers. As he traveled toward Jerusalem for worship, he certainly joined those around him in singing Psalm 122. "I was glad when they said to me, 'Let us go to the house of the Lord.'"

We have heard these words many times. Many a Sunday school teacher has explained them to young children, saying, "Going to church is what makes Christian people happy." This is a pleasant notion until we look around the sanctuary. In any given church, we may see frowns on teenagers, forced against their will to attend. Somebody may have a bone to pick with the sinner across the aisle. A few folks may look anxious or fearful that God has not paid enough attention to their prayers. And who knows if someone present wants to shake a fist at the preacher?

But for the Jew, the destination evoked a deep sense of gladness. They were going to the house of the Lord — the big house — the temple. They were going to the one and only spot on this planet where the holy one said, "Make me a house." The Jerusalem temple was where the story of God was celebrated and kept alive. All of God's dealings with the human race were recounted. God's redemptive works were remembered and renewed in rituals. The priests sacrificed pure animals to beg God's forgiveness of sin. The people gave freely of their goods to express their holy thanks and to extend a hand to the poor. The house of God was their memory and their hope. That was why it was the finest house in the city. It was God's house.

It is true that people can pray anywhere, and they often do. Wherever there is a need, the prayer is spoken. Yet there is something powerful and poignant about bringing those prayers to the one specific place described as God's home upon the earth. It was with deep gladness that they went to the house of the Lord.

As a Protestant Christian, I have often missed the same experience of a place. Protestants have their church buildings and those developed out of the synagogue movement following the time of Jesus. In the first century, ancient Israel had a central temple in Jerusalem, but the people had been widely scattered. When it became impractical or unfeasible to travel to Jerusalem for worship, Jewish faith was fed by many local centers of instruction and community. These were the synagogues, presided over by the Pharisees. Within them, believers heard God's instruction.

After the Roman Empire destroyed the temple in 70 AD, these congregational centers kept Jewish faith alive. They became the models for how Christian congregations began to function and flourish. Synagogues offered a central place for believers to gather, to mark the sabbath, to hear of God's words, and to encourage one another in the faith. All of us remain in this tradition as we declare, "God can be anywhere — even in a building like this."

And so, we mark our own personal Jerusalems. There are special places where things have happened, unique locations where God seems to have set foot. In the old section of Edinburgh, Scotland, people visit Saint Giles' Cathedral. It functioned for hundreds of years as a Roman church until 1559, when John Knox preached a stem-winding sermon to incite the Scots Reformation. His peers said of him, "John Knox is able in one hour to put more life in us than five hundred trumpets continually blasting our ear."

The pulpit is still there; the memory is still there. It was a most impressive place to visit, although the midday service that my wife and I attended there was deadly dull. Sitting in a very old pew, I found myself praying for the ghost of Knox to return and haunt us for a while.

Many of us visit and mark our places of spiritual significance. But this is not quite the same as going to Jerusalem. For the Jew, the holy city is of central importance. As Abraham Heschel, one of the most distinguished rabbis of the last century, once wrote,

> *For more than three thousand years, we have been in love with Jerusalem. She occupied our hearts, filled our prayers, and pervaded our dreams. Continually mourning her loss, our grief was not subdued when celebrating festivities, when arranging a dinner table, when painting our homes. No meal was concluded without imploring, "Build Jerusalem, speedily, in your own days."*[5]

It has always been that way. After an invading army once destroyed the holy city, one of Israel's poets sang the blues. "If I forget you, O Jerusalem, let my right hand wither! Let my tongue cling to the roof of my mouth, if I do not remember you, if I do not set Jerusalem above my highest joy!" (Psalm 137:5-6). Listen carefully — the emphasis is not merely on the pain of the city's destruction but on the threat of losing God's continuing interaction with God's people. Call it "covenant" or call it "communion" — but this is the key to our ultimate gladness. We want to keep connected with our God. Jerusalem is the symbol of that relationship.

I remember the first time I saw the holy city with my own eyes. It was a thrill. I had heard about Jerusalem for forty years. My third-grade Bible had pictures of it. My teachers told me stories about what had happened there. The Ten Commandments were

5 Abraham Heschel, Israel: *An Echo of Eternity* (New York: Farrar, Straus, & Giroux, 1967) 26.

A Glimpse Of The Destination

carried into Jerusalem in the Ark of the Covenant. King David built a palace, King Solomon built a temple. Jerusalem was the center of Jewish faith. The city was also the home of Christian faith. Jesus broke the communion bread in Jerusalem, prayed in Jerusalem, was crucified in Jerusalem, and was raised from the dead in Jerusalem. I could not wait to see the city for myself. As we came around the bend on the Mount of Olives, there it was — shimmering in the gold light of the brilliant sunshine.

This is not to say that the city is a peaceful place nor that it is perpetually reverent. Many modern pilgrims will see their share of cheap olive wood trinkets, hear some tour guides fabricating improbable stories, and observe young Israelis in military uniforms walking down the Via Dolorosa with irreverent machine guns.

At one point in my own journey, I stood in line at the Church of the Holy Sepulchre, the traditional site where Jesus was crucified and buried. It is a dark structure in the ancient part of Jerusalem. Like the Christian church, it is divided into sections with Catholic, Orthodox, and Armenian believers protecting their own pieces of it. It took an hour and a half to step along a dark staircase toward the place where the cross of Jesus was reportedly put into the ground. Just as I took my turn to insert my hand in a hole in the floor to touch the rock, a man with an Italian accent pushed me out of the way. He wanted his crippled son to kiss the spot in the hope of being healed. It was then that I saw a nearby pile of crutches no longer used by their owners.

"Well, wait a minute," I murmured. It was my turn and he was rude. I had waited forever for this moment — so had he. As I stood my ground, a cranky Armenian priest wagged his finger and motioned me out of there. Apparently, I had squandered my turn. It was infuriating until the deeper truth sank in: I had gone there as a tourist, ready to consume the moment and pose for a picture. The boy had been brought as a pilgrim, ready to be healed. He and his family had gone to that place to take God seriously and pray for restoration.

"I was glad when they said to me, 'Let us go to the house of the Lord.'" Jerusalem is more than a city. It is a symbol for how God meets humanity. The pilgrim goes to Jerusalem to pray and worship, to remember and to hope. God has done great things, and must be thanked. God is capable of doing great things, and must be approached in prayer. God can ground our life in grace and orient our days in fruitful pursuits; therefore God must be heard and worshiped. The Christian life is more than going to church out of habit; it is going out of gladness. It is traveling in the knowledge that we could be changed and shaped into something new. On every step of the pilgrim road, we turn to worship the God whom we will finally see face-to-face. As Eugene Peterson writes, "Worship does not satisfy our hunger for God — it whets our appetite. Our need for God is not taken care of by engaging in worship — it deepens. It overflows the hour and permeates the week."[6]

Worship is really not about any of us, but it is something that we do. "The tribes of the Lord go up to Jerusalem," said the singer of Psalm 122, "just as they were decreed." That is, they didn't have a choice. They were told to go. They had to go. They were commanded to worship, said the psalmist, commanded "to give thanks to the name of the Lord."

I realize this does not sound flexible to most of us, in a time when religious devotion is regarded as optional. However, in ancient Jerusalem, there were not a lot of choices on how to spend one's discretionary time. The city was built around the worship of God, and everybody was commanded to go. They

6 Eugene Peterson, *A Long Obedience in the Same Direction* (Downers Grove: Intervarsity Press, 1980) 52.

did not have a choice. There were no football scrimmages, soccer games, shopping mall sales, or home and garden stores — only the Jerusalem temple opened its doors. Those were simpler days, and every Jew was expected to go. It is not all that different from how Sunday life was observed by the Puritans and the Calvinists who came to this country.

In fact, this is not very different from the family in which I was raised. When Sunday morning came, we knew the routine. We got out of bed, cleaned ourselves up, put on uncomfortable shoes, and went to a sanctuary to sit still for an hour or so. Then we spent a second hour in Sunday school, where Mrs. Caswell made us memorize the verse, "I was glad when they said to me, 'Let us go to the house of the Lord.'"

At this point along my own pilgrim road, I am glad I was forced to do that. I am glad that, just like the people of Israel, I was commanded to worship whether I felt like it or not. I am glad that week after week, I was made to sit in a big open sanctuary where there were words written above the pipe organ, words that still read, "Enter into God's gates with thanksgiving."

Why am I glad? It is because that repeated experience of Christian worship shaped my life as it shaped the lives of those around me. None of us were left to our own whims, our own desires, our own descriptions of who we are. We did not have to follow the world's definitions of success or happiness, for we were told in worship that we are the children of God. God claimed us in the love of Jesus Christ, because God believes the whole world is worthy of costly and magnificent love.

Every week, like it or not, worship is what Christian people do, worship is where we go, worship is where we pray and sing and listen — until all thankfulness starts to sink in. If we go frequently enough, we will hear that Jesus calls us friends. We will learn the songs and stories of a God who sets us free from the destructive powers in our world, and these will shape us as the people of God and friends of Christ.

At the end of Psalm 122, the psalmist sang of the peace of God that is given to be shared by all people. The Hebrew word is "shalom," a word of mutual benefit. "Shalom" means that everything is balanced, that all hostility is cancelled. No one dominates at the expense of anyone else. The weak are not exploited. The powerful share what they have. The violent are neutralized, and all have access to the same power. This is "shalom," the peace of God.

All who worship God will discover this to be God's vision for the world. Scripture is full of what God dreams for us. The lion and the lamb dwell together in shalom. The elderly and the infant depend on one another. The rich and the poor stand side by side and no one goes hungry for bread. Sin is cancelled, restoration is received, and no one grabs or clutches more than anybody else. This is what God reveals in worship as the scriptures are heard and understood.

When you worship, said the psalmist, pray for this kind of peace, for this is what God wishes to work out among all people. Pray the whole city will be sound and secure, that every child will be safe, that every voice will be respected. As the apostle Paul wrote some centuries after the psalmist, "If one suffers, all suffer; if one rejoices, all rejoice."[7] This is how God's people are bound together for the benefit of all. Nowhere is the need greater than in a city like Jerusalem, torn and damaged by human sin, yet worthy of God's redemption.

The deep truth of the psalm is this: worship gives us a view of God's mission to the world. The more we worship, the more we see. And the more we see, the more we engage in what God wants to accomplish here around us and in the world. It is the

7 1 Corinthians 12:26.

A Glimpse Of The Destination

building up of shalom, and it will make us glad.

"I was glad when they said to me, 'Let us go to the house of the Lord.'" There is something about the work of worship that is good and beneficial for the world. So, we are invited to keep at it, week after week, not because we have to, but because God is at work in us. The work of God in our hearts is always accompanied by joy — more than fleeting happiness, more than mere obligation, but a deep and abiding sense that we are here to take part in what God is getting done.

Worship is good for us, and ultimately it is good for the world, for it points us toward God and reveals God's greater purposes. We catch a glimpse of where we are headed. Our final destination is to share in the gladness of God.

Reflection Questions

"A Glimpse Of The Destination," Psalm 122

— Where are the holy places in my life? How do they offer a preliminary glimpse of God?

— Have I ever taken a pilgrimage to an important spiritual destination?

— How did it feel when I first saw it? And what did I do with this feeling?

— Does the experience of worship give me any sense of gladness? Why or why not?

— Can I distinguish between the God that I worship, and the imperfect people who are with me in the moment?

— How do my own imperfections push me toward the grace of God?

— How does worship "whet our appetite for God"?

— In your own words, how would you describe God's intentions for human life?

The Scorn Of Those Who Are At Ease
A Song Of Ascents

To you I lift up my eyes,
  O you who are enthroned in the heavens!
As the eyes of servants look to the hand of their master,
  as the eyes of a maid to the hand of her mistress,
  so our eyes look to the LORD our God,
  until he has mercy upon us.
Have mercy upon us, O LORD, have mercy upon us,
  for we have had more than enough of contempt.
Our soul has had more than its fill
  of the scorn of those who are at ease,
  of the contempt of the proud.   (Psalm 123: 1-4)

There are fifteen psalms named as Songs of Ascent, and this is the fourth. Each is a signpost along the pilgrim road. They offer guidance and assurance, declaring the goodness of God and the worthiness of trust. Some of these psalms warn us about possible road hazards. Psalm 123 is brief, but it is offered as a big yellow "caution" sign. It says, "Watch With Care — Bumpy Road Ahead."

The experienced traveler knows that every journey bears the possibility of trouble. This is no surprise. In the psalm before us, the surprise is the source. Trouble can come from those who are "at ease."

"At ease…" that sounds like a military phrase. When soldiers are no longer standing at attention, they are "at ease." Their shoulders relax. Their postures soften. They stop worrying about standing in straight lines. When they return home, they put their feet up and lean back in comfort. They are "at ease."

The Pilgrim Road

Psalm 123 warns that people "at ease" will scorn anybody who wants to live a deeper faith in God. Or to put it another way, if you are serious about orienting your life toward God and moving more deeply into God's presence, do not be surprised if you catch some flak from people who are not so serious.

Some teenagers will see it on Saturday morning at church camp. It is the morning after the big campfire. All the campers circle up on the lawn. They sing and sway to one final song. They hold hands, pray, and will not let go. It has been a good week. Campers and counselors are excited about God. They see the promise of living as Christians. God's kingdom is so close that they can taste it.

Then all the minivans start rolling in. One indifferent parent after another says to each kid, "Let's get going. Get your duffel bag and put it in the car." The camp director wonders if faith will last until the end of the driveway.

Maybe you go to a conference. The speakers are wonderful. The room is charged with spiritual energy. You are so excited about what you have heard, so thrilled by what you have learned but when you return home, it is business as usual. Within an hour of returning, you fear you are going to lose everything you gained.

This is one of the road hazards on the pilgrim road. Say, for instance, you go on an intentional trip to help other people. Your eyes are opened. Your heart is pried open. You meet people in pain, and find a way to make a constructive difference. I watched a woman in my church weep openly as she held sick infants at a third world clinic. For a few important hours, her ministry was holding babies, many of whom would not survive the week.

She returned home, shaken and cracked open, and one coworker asked, "How was your vacation? Did you do anything fun?" He gave her about thirty seconds to talk about it before his eyes glazed over and he changed the subject. She found it difficult to share the excitement, the urgency, the fullness of such an experience with somebody who would not take the same trip.

It is particularly awkward to live the Christian life if the people around you are "at ease." It is not that they are enemies, per se; that topic will come up in another one of these psalms. No, these are not enemies. They are simply indifferent. At the beginning of the spiritual journey, one of the greatest difficulties is the indifference of people around us.

When I began my work as a pastor, there was a young man who lived with his grandparents, off the alley behind my home. I knew all of them as neighbors and the grandfather was technically a member of my congregation. He was actually more a member of the church alumni association than an active member. He showed up for an hour on Christmas and Easter, and that was about it.

In the mystery of God's providence, his grandson "got religion." The boy started reading his Bible and joined a prayer group. He put three or four new bumper stickers on the back of his Ford. It was obvious that not only he was a Christian, but that he was driving a Christian car.

One Thursday night, I took out the garbage and Grandpa was waiting for me in the alley. "Reverend," he said, "I think my grandson is going off the deep end."

I asked what was wrong. Grandpa said, "Michael is always talking about the Bible — he never used to do that, and he talks about what he's reading. He leaves the room if he doesn't like what we are watching on the television. Then he got involved in some other church, and he goes there all the time. Don't get me wrong, Reverend, religion is fine in small doses, but he's going overboard. I said to him, 'Calm down, Michael, we're Presbyterians.'"

The Pilgrim Road

"One night," said the grandfather, "my wife asked him to say a blessing at the dinner table. That was a mistake. He prayed until the potatoes got cold. After he finally said 'Amen,' I told my wife, 'Don't ever ask Michael to pray again.' Dang if he didn't start praying right then and there. He was asking God to save me, to redeem me, and it was embarrassing. I finally interrupted his prayer to say, 'Michael, would you please pass the meat loaf?' He kept praying. He wanted God to interrupt our meal."

Grandpa concluded, "Reverend, I don't know what to do. Religion is fine for the weak and the needy, but I think Michael is becoming a fanatic. Do you have any advice for me?"

I looked at him, not knowing what to say. My voice locks up at such moments. Then I blurted out something that I regretted for about five seconds. I said, "My advice is that you start going to church with your grandson." Then I walked back inside my house.

How do you explain faith to people who are "at ease"? I am not really sure it can be done. If God gets hold of us, if somehow God speaks to us, the hardest obstacle may be keeping a clear view around those who are spiritually lazy.

As the pilgrim moves toward God, she sings Psalm 123. She sings, 'I have had enough of the scorn of those who are proud. I have had my fill of the contempt of those who are at ease.' That is how the psalmist describes her situation: 'I have had my fill … I am saturated and stuffed… I am full-up and fed up with those who sneer at me.' And why do they sneer? Because their lives are all about comfort, ease, and taking pride in how important they are.

I do not know how a psalm like this plays in my neighborhood, where people manicure their lawns and pursue expensive vacations. I have learned that when you discover there is so much more to life than comfort and ease, you have to contend with people who criticize you from the chaise lounge.

Frederick Buechner told about a Sunday brunch at an elegant mansion on Long Island. He was a young, successful novelist, and to his surprise, he had a conversion experience while listening to a Presbyterian sermon. Through a lot of soul-searching and the kindly influence of a minister, Buechner enrolled in a seminary to study theology. It was a major change in his life's direction.

He described the long abundant table as cluttered with silver and crystal. The pleasant faces were affluent strangers. At the far end of the table, his slightly deaf grandmother spoke up and stopped all conversation. She said, "Frederick, I understand that you are planning to enter the ministry. Is this your own idea or have you been poorly advised?"[8] Everybody in the well-heeled crowd turned and looked at him, frozen in time. He claimed she meant no harm by saying this, but it was telling that it happened at the Sunday brunch table and not in the narthex of a church sanctuary.

There are a lot of people who do not understand what committed pilgrims do with their time or money. Perhaps they lack the courage to face the needs in their own souls. Maybe they are unwilling to move through their comfort and ease into the fiery presence of God. If the Christian life is a spiritual journey, they will not make the trip. It is simply too disruptive. The prospect of making a real journey compromises their sense of comfort. They may be afraid of how it will affect them.

I think of Macon Leary, a character in one of Anne Tyler's novels. He wrote travel guides for people who hate to travel, and he did it because he hated to travel himself. Macon did not like the disruptions of going anywhere new. So, he wrote for people who "pretend they had never left home." And what did he research

8 Frederick Buechner, *The Alphabet of Grace* (New York: Harper & Row Publishers, 1970), 41.

41

for his travel guides?

> *What hotels in Madrid boasted king-sized Beautyrest mattresses? What restaurants in Tokyo offered Sweet'n'Low? Did Amsterdam have a McDonald's? Did Mexico City have a Taco Bell? Did any place in Rome serve Chef Boyardee ravioli? Other travelers hoped to discover distinctive local wines; Macon's readers searched for pasteurized and homogenized milk.[9]*

One great temptation of the Christian spiritual journey is to remain "at ease" — to stick with what we know. To downgrade a real adventure to familiar patterns that will not challenge nor disrupt. If we give into this temptation, we will remain the way we were: insulated, isolated, and distant from God.

The Christian life is hard work. Loving people is hard work. Forgiving people is hard work. Telling the truth is hard work. Giving up all worldly attachments and living more simply is hard work. Turning away from all our toys and toward God is hard work. Christian faith is not for sissies.

Some people understand this, even if it is met with resistance. A while back, a wedding was held at my church. The families were not members of the congregation, but they seemed very pleasant. Like all of the weddings I have ever seen, the bride was beautiful, the groom was handsome. The plans were elaborate and the bridal party spent piles of money on everything except the clergy.

A few days before the wedding, the bride's mother called the church office in a horrified voice. "The bride has broken her leg," she announced. "What were we going to do?"

Well, "we" could not do anything except pray. The broken leg became a family emergency. Everybody was notified. Anxiety was high. The mother feared that the dress had to be altered. Actually, it was fine, but a seamstress was called in, just in case.

9 Anne Tyler, *The Accidental Tourist* (New York: Albert P. Knopf, 1985), 11.

The Scorn Of Those Who Are At Ease

When the big day arrived, a neighboring Episcopalian priest stood with me to conduct the service. He preached the sermon, and it was memorable. He looked at the hobbling bride and said, "The true mark of love is a willingness to suffer. We suffer willingly for those we love. We suffer willingly *with* those we love. In its truest form, love is a giving up of pretension and comfort. Love is voluntarily entering into the painful experience of those you care about."

From where I stood, it was clear the bride's parents did not appreciate that sermon. The mother's eyes glazed over and she popped another antidepressant. The father's cheeks turned ruby red, and he looked like he was ready to explode. I am happy to report that the bride and groom took the sermon to heart, and they remain happily married.

Sadly, there is more to the story. After the ceremony, the bride's father verbally attacked the priest in the parking lot. Because of that sermon, the father had demanded back the check for the honorarium, which he ripped into small pieces in front of the priest before driving away in a limousine. I heard about this stunt a few minutes later as the priest returned to pick up his robe. I offered to split with him the forty bucks I had received. He glanced at the cross on our communion table, smiled slyly, and said, "No, that's all right. It goes with the territory."

Remember the psalmist's complaint? "We have had more than enough of the contempt. Our soul has had more than its fill of the scorn of those who are at ease." There is something more demanding to spiritual growth than playing it safe. We cannot move into God's presence by taking it easy or sugarcoating the truth of the gospel.

Those who pray this psalm look up. They lift their eyes above the voices around them. They raise their sights above the voices of comfort and ease. They peer to see the throne that is so high and lofty that only God is worthy to sit upon it. As they look up, they remember who they are — not masters of spiritual maturity, but servants of the living God. They do not call the shots or determine the mission, for that is God's role. And they do not have to concede anything to the amateur critics who are too lazy to join them for the journey.

Three times the pilgrim cries to God for mercy. Mercy, mercy, mercy! The prayer is aimed toward the one whose grace is sufficient for us. We are servants of God, not masters of our own domains. That is the key distinction that sets us free. We find our true selves through service, sacrificing all control needs, and looking toward the generous hand of God.

The Christian life is not an easy life. It is a cross-shaped life, shaped by sacrifice and commitment. This is one of the open secrets when we get in step on the pilgrim road. The *happy church* will not admit this as they mimic the world's counterfeit values of success and me-first fulfillment. In the *establishment church* that prides itself in attracting the who's who of Main Street, they will probably water down this truth. The church does not always tell us how hard it will be to follow Jesus after we have been converted, confirmed, or ordained.

So here is an essential truth for the spiritual journey: the world that resists God does not cheer us on as we move toward God. The powers-that-be are too invested in the way things are to ever consider the disruptive power of the gospel. The people who are most comfortable in this world will almost always wrinkle their noses at the citizens of heaven. That is just the way it is.

This is exactly as Jesus warned us. "The word of God is like a seed," he said, "and sometimes it falls among thorns that choke it and kill it." These thorns, he said, "are the cares of the world, the lure of wealth, and the desire for other things..."[10] It is sad to say,

10 Mark 4:19.

The Scorn Of Those Who Are At Ease

but for some people, death is their only wake-up call.

Read the road sign and take caution. And keep looking higher. Keep looking towards that throne and praying for mercy — traveling mercy. Keep looking and praying, praying and looking, until you see clearly that God is a lot kinder to us than the world is.

Reflection Questions

"The Scorn Of Those Who Are At Ease," Psalm 123

— Who are the people in my life who scoff at my spiritual journey?

— Can I identify people, perhaps closest to me, who resist my continuing growth?

— When did I discover that the Christian faith is hard work?

— When have I wanted to coast and take it easy?

— What in my spiritual journey is the hardest work for me to do?

— From what sources do I draw my strength and support for following Jesus?

— How does the cross of Christ provide both an example and a comfort for my faith?

— Why does the world resist its own redeemer?

If Not, Then...

A Song Of Ascents

If it had not been the LORD who was on our side
— let Israel now say —
if it had not been the LORD who was on our side,
when our enemies attacked us,
then they would have swallowed us up alive,
when their anger was kindled against us;
then the flood would have swept us away, the torrent would have
gone over us;
then over us would have gone the raging waters.
Blessed be the LORD, who has not given us as prey to their teeth.
We have escaped like a bird from the snare of the fowlers;
the snare is broken, and we have escaped.
Our help is in the name of the LORD, who made heaven and earth.

(Psalm 124: 1-7)

It was a foggy Saturday morning in July. Three friends were on their way to a music festival in upstate New York. I was the one snoozing in the back seat. Jack, a quiet engineering student from Colgate University, was our navigator. Donnie had volunteered to drive. It was just as well. He was not somebody who shared the wheel anyway. Prone to be pushy and arrogant, he would get us there in plenty of time.

We had not seen Donnie in over a year. He had gone to Columbia University and never looked over his shoulder. Once he phoned to say how he loathed small town life and Manhattan had opened up his world. "In fact," he said, "I'm not the same person that I used to be."

We did not know what he meant, but pretty soon we found

out. Somewhere on the outskirts of Oneonta, he said to Jack, "Could you do me a favor? Open the glove compartment and hand me that plastic bag." It was a bag of white powder. He began to carefully pour a thin line of cocaine on the dashboard of his car. He snorted it in a way that proved he had clearly done this before.

The transformation was frightening. His facial features became monstrous. He accelerated from 65 to 80, and the old car began to shiver. When Jack and I exclaimed, "What are you doing?" Donnie laughed and began mocking us. He refused to pull over and he would not slow down.

Pretty soon, it was clear that neither verbal persuasion nor outright confrontation would help. I was helpless in the backseat as this mad man started playing games behind the wheel. It was one of the most frightening moments in my life. He serpentined through the lanes, whooping as if he was having fun. I prayed for the police to pull us over and then thought better of it. Either he would speed up to avoid them, making things worse, or else I might end up in a jail cell with this idiot who was surely going to kill us.

Jack and I had to concoct a quick plan. I found a napkin on the floor, so I scribbled a clandestine note and slipped it to Jack around the side of the seat. "There is an exit coming up," I wrote. "Let's tell him we want breakfast." It was about 9:30 in the morning, so we convinced him to pull into a fast food place for a quick bite and a rest room stop. As we got out of the car, I grabbed Donnie in a wrestling hold while Jack grabbed his keys and ran away. He broke free from my full nelson, turned, and punched me in the stomach. Meanwhile Jack had thrown the car keys into a nearby dumpster, only to find out from the echo that it was empty.

No matter. Donnie started screaming at us and we screamed

back. We were not going anywhere with him. It did not matter how much the concert tickets cost. We sat on the curb, refusing to move until he flushed his baggie down the restaurant toilet and consented to let one of us drive. It took him a while to settle down and give in, but a couple of hours later, with Jack behind the wheel, we resumed our journey.

There are some stories that you never tell your parents and there are some stories they never told us. If we were to recount all the dangers that we have survived, it would probably frighten our loved ones to death. But we are survivors of more near-disasters than any of us would admit. The fifth psalm of ascent reminds us how we have gotten through the many dangers, toils, and snares thus far on our spiritual journeys.

"Our help is in the name of the Lord, who made heaven and earth." This famous Bible verse concludes a psalm about help. It affirms that God's help is what saves us in the face of trouble. 'If it hadn't been for God's invisible hand,' said the psalmist, 'we would have been swallowed alive. The flood would have swept us away. The waters would have overtaken us.' Obviously, this is not a psalm that everybody can sing. It does not explain why floods swallow up some and leave others high and dry. That is an issue for the philosophers. Psalm 124 is a psalm for survivors... for people like you and me.

The fact that we have lived to tell about such things is proof that God has carried us through a lot of difficulties and disruptions. As a pastor, I look out from my pulpit on any given Sunday to see recovering alcoholics, former sufferers of abuse, victims of crime, recovering drug addicts, released convicts, divorce survivors, those once diagnosed with depression, people who fell into financial debt, folks whose tempers have gotten them into trouble, and people who have had significant medical challenges — just to name a few.

The Pilgrim Road

When Sunday comes, all of us who go to church put our best face forward and try not to let the crooked stitches show. It is church, after all, and we really do hope to look respectable. But the truth is far grittier. We are those who have been rescued. Just below the veneer of respectability, every one of us has stories of how, somehow, in some way, God snatched us out of the jaws of some deadly beast. No matter how much we scrub up our appearances, we know that, but if not for the grace of God, life could have been a lot different for us. If we scrape away our delusions of self-sufficiency, all of us have "saving stories."

In my church building, there is a group of people who gather at 7:00 each morning to tell how they were rescued from the deadly power of alcohol. They remember how they identified the danger, how they came to terms with it, how they fought it, how they still struggle against its power, how they keep working to reclaim what it took from them. At the heart of it, they talk about the ways God gives them strength, courage, and forgiveness.

God is our helper — that is the overwhelming affirmation of Psalm 124. Sure, the psalm stops short of describing how God comes to help. It does not presume to define what God does or will do. Psalm 124 is Jewish enough to respect God's sneaky ways. God's dramatic rescues may be subtle enough that they are just below the radar. Perhaps God miraculously kept a falling tree from striking us or God gave us the momentary courage to take the car keys away from a drug-crazed friend. It might not have appeared to be a deeply spiritual moment at the time.

But there is no question of God's ultimate intent: to hold onto us, to keep us within the covenant community. The psalmist speaks in metaphors to describe the threats: floods, raging waters, a bird catcher's net. The troubles out there are real — but they will not swallow us, snare us, or sweep us away.

Of all the Bible writers, the one who echoed these thoughts was

If Not, Then...

a rabbi named Paul. His faith was shaped by praying the psalms. He kept hanging on to God as he went through an impressive list of troubles and the reason he did it was because he believed that God kept hanging on to him. That conviction prompted him to declare, "We know that all things work together for good for those who love God, who are called according to God's purpose."[11] This was his interpretation of the Hebrew words from another favorite psalm, that "goodness and mercy pursue me all the days of my life" (Psalm 23:6).

We can affirm such things when we tell the big "saving stories" of our faith. For the people of Israel, the greatest story was the exodus. After a lingering show-down with the king of Egypt, the king of the universe set his people free. God led them to a great sea and then split it wide open by blowing upon it. God's people walked through on dry land and then the sea closed up right behind them. They were free from their oppression and slavery.

For the church, the new Israel, the big "saving story" happened during the same week that Israel celebrates the exodus. An innocent man was condemned by the guilty, executed by those thirsty for blood, and then he took all of their guilt and hostility to his grave — where he buried it. When the sabbath was over, God raised him back to life, and put him on the throne where he rules the universe with wounded hands.

That final detail may be the one to remember. We remember not merely Christ's power, but his vulnerability. The Christian faith is the only faith that has a wounded Savior at its center. The very one who rules the world does so with pierced hands and a crown of thorns. The news may be embarrassing in a town like mine, where so many people aspire to be successful, yet it must be announced anyway: life is not about being strong, capable, and independent. Life is about receiving help from the only true

11 Romans 8:28.

51

source of help. We cannot make it down the pilgrim road on our own power. No matter how hard we try, we need help.

The apostle Paul preached this paradox all the time. Remember what he wrote in his letter to the Romans? "While we were still weak, Christ died for the ungodly.... While we were still sinners, Christ died for us."[12] When we could not help ourselves, Christ gave himself up to help us.

This reveals one of the greatest spiritual challenges for our Christian journey. We must learn how to receive help. It is bloody difficult for many of us to allow that. We say we do not want to put anybody else out, but we secretly believe that we can handle it ourselves, thank you very much. It is embarrassing to appear vulnerable. We do not want anybody to know we have difficulties. The teenager goes into a rehab program, and the parents keep it a secret, choosing to suffer in loneliness. The capable mother hen that looks in on everybody in need pushes away the people who want to look in on her. The business leader who has lived with incredible competence will do whatever he can to keep others from seeing that his mind is slipping.

"Help? I don't need any help. I can handle it myself."

Let me address these words to the strong and capable. If we live long enough, we will end our lives in the same way we began them — by depending on others. In between, it is difficult for us to admit whenever we need some help. It is almost as if we are saying, "I don't need God or anybody else, I can handle it myself." Pride is the first of the seven deadly sins. It is an arrogant master and it can enslave us.

There is no good news in a gospel of self-sufficiency. If we think we are self-sufficient, all we are left with is ourselves. None of us is strong enough to last. None of us is capable enough to always get it right. Our lives are limited, finite, with only so many

12 Romans 5: 6, 8

days, only so much strength, only so much health. Sooner or later every one of us will need help from beyond ourselves — and that is when it helps to have a God with all the wisdom and power of the universe in those holy, wounded hands.

"Our help is in the name of the Lord, who made heaven and earth." God is the creative one. Is God all-powerful? Yes, but not in a domineering way and certainly not in an obvious way. God is creative and can make a path where there was no path. God is creative and can make something beautiful in the middle of a wretched mess. God is creative, and creativity is all about problem-solving. The problem may be bigger than us, and sometimes it is God's ingenuity that gives us the most help.

But here is the important thing. We have to ask for help and learn to welcome it when it comes.

In what may be the classic "helping story" of the Bible, Jesus spun a tale about a man who stopped along a dangerous road to help a traveler in trouble. The victim had been beaten severely, robbed, left for dead, and passed by two religious leaders. Then a good Samaritan stopped to help. It is such a famous story that we do not understand it. The usual explanation is to reduce it to a morality lesson and declare how important it is to help our neighbors.

But that is not the true power of the story. It is told from the perspective of the victim of the robbery. As the victim lies in the ditch, watching the "love your neighbor" experts pass him by, the person who actually stopped to help was the last person any first-century Jew would expect. The helper was a Samaritan — an ugly, unwanted outcast. Yet he stopped with unrequested sympathy. Then he emptied his own pockets to assist the wounded traveler. He never asked permission to help; he crossed that invisible barrier and did what he could to the person in need.

Meanwhile, do you remember what the wounded traveler

does? He did nothing. The only appropriate response of the traveler was to receive the help. All he could do was lie there, permit somebody else to dress his wounds, and welcome the care of another. That is a hard lesson to learn, yet it may be the holiest lesson of all.

After Hurricane Katrina smashed the Gulf Coast in 2005, thousands of people went to help in whatever way they could. I was blessed to serve briefly on one of the rebuilding teams from my congregation. It is nearly impossible to describe the wreckage to those who saw only the television pictures. Buildings were flattened by wind and wave. Homes were swamped and mildewed. The region was decimated and many neighborhoods were unsafe after dark. When I rented a minivan for our team, I was stunned to discover it had a bullet hole through the passenger door. I dutifully went back inside to report this to the rental office and the lady behind the counter told me in great detail how it happened. That didn't instill much confidence in our team.

Later that week, my friend John was riding with me as we returned to our work site at rush hour. As we sped along Interstate 10, the front right tire hit a roofing nail and blew out. We pulled off the road. As I yanked out the tire jack and the spare, a good Samaritan stopped to help. At least he looked like a Samaritan: scraggly beard, stained shirt, dirty fingernails. He was quiet and focused and did not waste any words on us. He drove a panel truck with Maryland license plates and casually mentioned this was the seventh time he had driven a truck full of supplies to the region.

He jumped in without even asking. I said, "Thanks, but we can handle it." He was already on his knees, twisting off the lug nuts. Within a few minutes, the tire was changed and the jack was put away. The stranger refused any money, announcing, "I came down here to help whoever I met. On some days, I get to help the helpers." Then he wiped his hands on his dirty overalls and drove off quickly. We never did catch his name.

John and I climbed back into the car and started it up. After a mile or two of silence, he said, "You don't suppose that was Jesus, do you?"

I smiled and said, "We never know. After all, he *did* look like a good Samaritan."

"Our help is in the name of the Lord, who made heaven and earth." Sometimes the hardest thing in the world is to ask for help, to pray for help, or to receive help.

Yet help comes every moment of every day, in so many ways. It is a really good thing God does not wait to be asked.

Reflection Questions

"If Not, Then…," Psalm 124

— Can I name a situation where God seemed to rescue me?

— What was a risky, dangerous moment of my life that comes to mind?

— How is God involved in those occasions when I take my own rescue into my own hands?

— A favorite hymn sings, "Through many dangers, toils, and snares, I have already come." Can I name some of these — and reflect on how I have survived thus far?

— Which of these dangers was a learning experience for me? What have I learned?

— When have I resisted help from other people?

— What kind of practical help could I use right now?

— What does the weakness and ultimate crucifixion of Jesus reveal to me about God?

— What saving hope do I have as I consider Jesus' resurrection?

Where The Crooked Path Leads
A Song Of Ascents

*Those who trust in the LORD are like Mount Zion, which cannot
be moved, but abides forever.*
As the mountains surround Jerusalem,
*so the LORD surrounds his people, from this time on and
forevermore.*
*For the scepter of wickedness shall not rest on the land allotted to
the righteous,*
*so that the righteous might not stretch out their hands to do
wrong.*
*Do good, O LORD, to those who are good, and to those who are
upright in their hearts.*
*But those who turn aside to their own crooked ways the LORD
will lead away with evildoers.*
Peace be upon Israel!   (Psalm 125: 1-5)

The news reports said there were two thousand people in the
bookstore parking lot. It was widely touted as the midnight event
of the summer. All kinds of people were dressed up for it. There
were witches and wizards, a goblin or two, and a number of them
came in costumes. Many of the people around the bookstore had
a crooked scar painted on their foreheads. It was the night when
the seventh and final Harry Potter novel was released for millions
of readers.

Those who do not read scoffed and stayed home. They said,
"It's only a book" and stayed home to let the television think for
them. Sure, it is a book — but this best-selling series of children's
books are instant classics that have set well-deserved sales
records.

The Pilgrim Road

Others declared this was the latest in a series of books that are contrary to the teachings of the Bible. I respectfully disagree, because I have read all the books and seen all of the movies. I have reflected on them in light of scripture texts, such as the one that begins this chapter. That is a good bit more than can be said of the silly old men who have denounced them.

Here is why I begin this way: the Harry Potter books are about the struggle between good and evil. Each successive book describes a world growing increasingly darker. As we read through each book, there is an increase in meanness, betrayal, and destruction. For those who have not read the series, here is a spoiler alert: a lot of people get hurt and die.

Yet against the backdrop of evil, there is also a corresponding increase in goodness. In each book, good people take courage, band together for friendship and support, and use their ingenuity to resist everything that threatens to harm or enslave their world.

So here is my hunch why two thousand people went to a bookstore on a summer night. It was not only to buy a book. They wanted to know how the seven-volume story turns out. They wanted to know that goodness will win over evil.

In fact, I did my own informal poll as my daughter and I wound our way through the long line. About a third of those who walked out of the store were sneaking a peek at the back of the book. Before a literary purist yells out loud, take note of what these people were doing. They were checking to make sure that the story turned out all right. Only then could they start at the beginning and read the whole book.

All of us want to know that the journey will turn out well. There is nothing new about that. You can find such thinking in the Bible, the one book that still outsells the Harry Potter series. Our sixth psalm of ascent is about goodness triumphing over evil. Psalm 125 is a song of confidence. It is a prayer for ordering

Where The Crooked Path Leads

the world.

As we make our spiritual journey with the psalms, we recall how some psalms express confusion and difficulty. They pray honestly in the midst of disruption and disorder. The psalmist will ask, 'Lord, where are you? You said that you loved us, so why do we have so much trouble?'

But Psalm 125 is fixed and unmovable. It declares those who live the pilgrim life are firmly established. They are like a mountain that cannot be moved. They are like a great city surrounded by its defender. And how can it be otherwise? In the psalm immediately before this one, there is the great affirmation about God: "Our help is in the name of the Lord, who made heaven and earth." Biblical faith is all about God. If we peek ahead to the Bible's conclusion, all is well and everybody is singing. But it will be a bumpy ride to arrive there.

What this particular psalm adds is a description of the relationship that God has with his people. It is a reciprocal relationship: the people trust in the Lord, the Lord surrounds his people. Those who trust the Lord will endure forever, as the Lord embraces his people forever. There is no give and take necessary in this description. On the surface, it sounds like a perfect equation. If that were the case, we could say "shalom" to one another and get on with our perfect day.

But then there arises a well-known word that we do not use much anymore. It sticks out like a pebble in the oatmeal. Everything was so sweet and trusting as the psalm begins, until the composer of the song says the word "wickedness." When was the last time you used that word?

We remember stories about "wicked witches" of east and west, but these days "wicked" has lost its moral edge. Two skateboarders were comparing a jump and called it "wicked." It had a sharper edge than calling it "extreme." Or perhaps the

59

The Pilgrim Road

NASCAR announcer said the track had a "wicked" turn. That might mean it had a "nasty" turn — but the track designer probably didn't mean to be cruel, only challenging.

By contrast, the word for wickedness has to do with intentional evil. It has to do with corrupting and destroying human life.

Evil is a constant presence among us, and blessed are those who see it clearly. In recent years, the Roman Catholic Archdiocese of Los Angeles settled a $660 million dollar suit. They acknowledged that children had been abused by a few of their church leaders, and admitted the church had ignored its victims and moved the perpetrators to other parishes without punishment. A priest spoke up for the pope, apologized with honest regret, and said, "We have to acknowledge and deal with the *wickedness* in our own ranks."[13] They are not alone in that.

Wickedness — we don't often use that word. But if our spiritual journey is aimed toward loving God and loving our neighbor, we begin to see wickedness. Recall some of the snapshots that we have seen in the evening news:

- It is wickedness to bomb a village where there are innocent children, and it is wickedness to intentionally move children into the path of enemy fire and to film it for propaganda purposes.

- It is wickedness to spend the pension funds that your employees have earned, and it is wickedness to indebt your grandchildren so you can live in comfort.

- It is wickedness to destroy something that is not yours, and it is wickedness to torture people when you cannot prove they did anything wrong.

13 http://news.yahoo.com/s/nm/20070717/wl_nm/priests_abuse_vatican_dc

Where The Crooked Path Leads

- It is wickedness to eat a full meal in the presence of those who starve and it is wickedness to build a casino that will draw in the underemployed and take their money.

Even the secular dictionary *Wikipedia* concedes that wickedness "refers to human sin," not merely as our corrupt or weakened condition, but our deliberate choice to do evil over doing good. To gossip about somebody as a way of making yourself look better — that is wicked. To perpetuate a false story that keeps you in power — that is wicked, too. To economically enslave a race of people so we can have cheap cotton or to exploit another person for our gain — that is wicked.

If the Christian life is a journey toward God, the psalmist wants us to do some moral housecleaning on our way. We are prompted to deal with those situations where we have fallen into the baser desires of the soul. That is how the New International Version translates the Hebrew text: "The scepter of the wicked will not remain over the land allotted to the righteous, for then the righteous might use their hands to do evil" Psalm 125:3(NIV). It is not merely the "bad people" who do bad things, it is the good people who do nothing or, worse, give in to corruption. That is where those of us on the pilgrim road have to take responsibility, make different choices, and turn ourselves toward a kinder, more generous, and more just direction.

To put it in the words of the psalm, whose scepter is going to rule over you? Are you going to be governed by the powers of good or the powers of evil? This is really the perpetual human question. Sadly, we never graduate beyond it. The struggle between good and evil is on our path every day.

Sometimes people talk about moral progress, but I have no evidence that it is anything more than a vain dream. There is no technological advancement to make us more humane; if anything, we make bigger and more efficient artillery. There is no psychological development that moves anybody beyond the possibility of corruption. There is no social policy that will make us more kind, nor is there an economic policy that will make us more generous. Somebody always has something that others do not have, and nobody stays content with that.

The longer I live, the more I doubt that human progress is ever really possible. Any attempt to improve ourselves only seems temporary. The folks in my congregation stop by regularly to tell of some of the messes that they have fallen into. When it comes to getting into trouble, most people are quite a creative bunch.

And that is why we need this psalm. It reminds us that not only will our pursuit of perfection never perfect the world — it will not come close to perfecting us. As much as the psalm calls us away from the power of evil, it reminds us that it is not our goodness that matters most. It is God's goodness. It is finally up to God to make everything turn out well.

Because God is good, because God stays with us regardless of whether we are good, all things are finally held in God's beneficent hands. We have peeked ahead to the last page and discovered God's story will turn out all right — and that is what allows us to take stock of our own moral situation. In the confidence that God's good rule will banish the scepter of wickedness, we can keep choosing to be as good as we possibly can.

Along the way, the psalmist offers only one line of prayer in this song: "Do good, O Lord, to those who are good." He has no prayer for those on the crooked path, for that is not God's path. The crooked path is a detour — it is the original *highway to nowhere*. Since there is a God of goodness who calls us, surrounds us, and inevitably meets us, the journey is really God's journey. Whether we pave it with good intentions or good deeds, it is

Where The Crooked Path Leads

finally God's goodness that gets us to where we are going. And it is God's goodness that gives us the power to leave all detours and return to the paths of righteousness.

The guidance of Psalm 125 is quite simple. If you are doing something destructive in your life, cut it out. If you are doing something good, let it grow. Do not spend a lot of energy fretting about your worthiness. Instead, invest in the goodness of the God who loves you as much as he loves everybody else.

In the end, the final word in this psalm is "shalom." Peace be to Israel! Or to translate this in a way we can understand: "Chill out." Our lifelong journey of faith is in God's hands. We keep praying for God to be good to those who are good — and in the process, the prayer begins to shape our practice. We lean forward toward God, love every neighbor around us, and ultimately we find ourselves among the beloved of God. It is exactly where we belong.

Reflection Questions

"Where The Crooked Path Leads," Psalm 125

— What frightens me most?

— When have I seen something or someone that I would classify as "wicked"?

— Are there whims, hungers, or behaviors that threaten to destroy me?

— When has my life been saved by the decisions that I have made?

— How do I think God will ultimately remove evil from the world? Will this be a gradual process or an abrupt intervention?

— Can I trust God to be good?

— What are some intentional decisions that I could make to reject evil; To move toward what is good?

Consumed By Joy

A Song Of Ascents

When the LORD restored the fortunes of Zion, we were like those who dream.
Then our mouth was filled with laughter, and our tongue with shouts of joy;
then it was said among the nations, "The LORD has done great things for them."
The LORD has done great things for us, and we rejoiced.
Restore our fortunes, O LORD, like the watercourses in the Negeb.
May those who sow in tears reap with shouts of joy.
Those who go out weeping, bearing the seed for sowing,
shall come home with shouts of joy, carrying their sheaves.

(Psalm 126: 1-6)

When Dr. Bruce Metzger died some years ago, the *New York Times* called him one of the foremost American Bible scholars of the twentieth century. He taught at Princeton Theological Seminary for 45 years and, after he retired, he kept hanging around the library. Dr. Metzger led the translation team that prepared the New Revised Standard Version of the Bible, as well as four editions of the translation that preceded it. He knew the Bible well enough to have near-perfect recall of everything within it. Back in seminary, I was fortunate to study with him for two classes and there was one moment I will never forget.

Class had concluded one day and Dr. Metzger was straightening his lecture notes. A student went up and said, "Dr. Metzger, I have to preach for a real live congregation next Sunday and I told them that my text was from Paul's letter to the Philippians. Do you have any tips on what I should say?" It sounded like a

The Pilgrim Road

hopelessly general question from an inexperienced preacher, but the professor took it in stride.

He thought for a moment and said, "Talk about joy. The Greek word for 'joy' appears in various forms fourteen times in that brief letter. Paul wanted to reinforce the importance of joy as a primary theme of the Christian life. Joy is simply that important. Have a good day." He smiled and was gone.

If our eyes are open, we quickly notice that joy is a word that comes up again and again in the Bible. As we travel the pilgrim road, sooner or later we need to talk about joy. It is the gravitational center of Psalm 126. Joy surfaces four times in the six verses of our psalm. "Our mouth was filled with laughter, and our tongue with shouts of joy... the Lord has done great things for us, and we rejoiced!" (Psalm 126:2-3).

I can imagine these psalm verses swirling inside the apostle Paul's head as he sat in a Roman prison cell. Suddenly, he may have banged his tin cup against the bars and shouted, "Can you bring me pen and paper? I need to write a letter to those Philippians." While the other prisoners were complaining about the oatmeal, Paul wrote, "Rejoice in the Lord always; again, I say rejoice."[14]

The scene, which is probably quite close to true, brings up a recurring question: how do we explain a person like that? He had every reason to grumble about his situation, but he hummed a hymn. He had every reason to ask for help, but he said, "I'm quite content." He had every reason to feel anger, resentment, and the need to retaliate — but instead he said, "Rejoice!"

This is a reminder that joy is not the same thing as happiness. Happiness depends on our circumstances. Are we having a good day? Are the children turning out as we had hoped? Do we have food on the table? Is there money in the bank? Do we feel a sense

14 Philippians 4:4

of purpose about our days? If so, chances are we are probably happy and not sad.

By contrast, joy is a quality of life that comes, even when the circumstances of our situations are not turning out very well. We hear a trace of this in Psalm 126. The specific line of prayer is verse four: "Restore our fortune, O Lord, like the watercourses of the Negeb." Apparently life has dried up for the psalmist, as if she were in the Negeb desert. So the psalmist begins to pray for a flash flood.

Perhaps it came, for the psalm moves toward a double blessing. "May those who sow in tears reap in shouts of joy! May those who go out weeping, bearing the seed for sowing, come home with shouts of joy!" Take note that they have the seed — joy is that seed. Regardless of their tears, the seed can always take root and grow. In spite of how tough things can be, joy can still come to us. It is a gift of God, given to those who trust that our circumstances are completely in the hands of a God who loves us.

Before the Christians caught on to this, it was first a Jewish idea. Jews have always known that it is possible to be joyful when we are solemn. Joy remains with us even in the midst of difficulty, particularly if it is rooted in our memory. Nothing ever happens quickly in the Jewish scriptures. The Jews were enslaved for a generation or two in Egypt before God set them free. They wandered for forty years in the desert before they arrived at the promised land. They were exiled to Babylon for about fifty years before God sent them home.

As the Jews have always understood, joy is possible if we take the long view. God saved us in the past, and God will save us again. In between comes the prayer of Psalm 126: 'So save us now, Lord, like a flash flood in the desert!' The memory, the hope, the prayer — these are the gifts that joy keeps alive. They also prepare us to receive joy when it comes.

The Pilgrim Road

When I was a teenager, I never knew about this long-term, stick-it-out dimension of joy. Then the advisors of my church youth group announced they were planning a Passover Seder. They said a rabbi would be with us and it would be a joyful event. The minister's son showed up with a box of yarmulkes for us to wear. As goofy teenage Protestants, we thought that was cool. The Seder began and the rabbi made us stick to its long script. We drank four cups of grape juice, sampled a tablespoon of horseradish, hunted for hidden matzoh, and prayed for freedom for all Jews. The evening went on for a while, but the whole event struck me as rather serious. What kind of joy was this?

Of course, as a Presbyterian I should have known better. How many times did I see a minister stand behind the communion table and intone, "This is the joyful feast of the people of God." Nobody ever said, "Whoopee!" The sacraments of my childhood may have been quiet, reverent, and reflective — but remembering the Lord's death was never "happy." Yet it was joyful, as I now understand, because God was doing something in and through the death of Jesus. Specifically, God was doing something in us. We were being saved from our human slavery to sin and death. That is the origin of spiritual joy.

There is a profound difference between "happiness" and "joy." We often let the two words run together, but there is an important distinction between them. Happiness is circumstantial; It is hit or miss. But joy is what happens within us, regardless of what is happening outside us. Paul puts joy high on his list of the fruits of the Holy Spirit, second only to love.[15] It seems that when God starts working within us in the invisible power of Christ, we will first be filled with love and then filled with joy.

We do not know the circumstances that prompted Psalm 126. How was it that God restored the people's fortunes? The specific

15 Galatians 5:22

details have long been forgotten, even as the memory remains. In his translation of the first verse, Eugene Peterson tied the psalm to the return of Zion's exiles.[16] Perhaps that was the big event the travelers remembered. After decades of being far from home as captives in Babylon, God brought them back to Israel. If so, it was probably a communal memory of something the people did not experience first-hand. Yet they knew in their bones that God was restoring what the world had taken away from them. That memory was brought into the present tense as they prayed for God to free them once again.

It is this "already but not yet" quality that gives joy its sustaining power. We remember what God has done and expect to see it again. There is an incongruity between the memory and the expectation. Sometimes it is downright comical. A good bit of the Jewish humor that emerged in the Catskills is rightly directed at a holy God who makes promises that wait to be completely fulfilled. One scholar observed this discontinuity as the engine for much Jewish humor. In the words of filmmaker Woody Allen, "If it turns out that there is a God, I don't think that he is evil. I think that the worst thing you could say is that he is, basically, an underachiever."[17]

Good humor has always been a mark of God's faithful. One of the funniest people in church history was a young nun who was born almost five hundred years ago. She lived in Spain and her name was Teresa of Avila. The church named her Saint Teresa, but there were some in her day who thought she was not holy enough.

Once she was having a bad day, riding in a carriage across a stream. The axle broke and she tumbled into the mud. She cried

16 Psalm 126 in The Message (Colorado Springs: Nav Press, 1993).
17 "Love and Death," directed by Woody Allen (1975; Beverly Hills, California: United Artists).

out toward heaven, "O Lord, if this is how you treat your friends, it is no wonder that you have so few of them."

She was a holy woman who wrote important books on prayer and the spiritual life. Teresa lived during the difficult days of the Spanish Inquisition. Church people could freely accuse one another of distorting the faith and punishment broke out everywhere. Meanwhile, Saint Teresa prayed in her cloister, "Lord, deliver me from sour-faced saints."

Once she was accused of eating too joyfully during Lent. She looked up from her plate to answer, "There is a time for penance, and a time for partridge."

Then she instructed the sisters of her order to dance in the monastery. "But do it," she said, "when the outsiders aren't looking."

As preacher Fred Craddock once said, "The surest sign that the grace of God is at work in a person's life is a sense of humor." We want that, don't we?

Churches say they want that. In the back of Christian magazines, we can see the advertisements: "We are looking for a minister: seven years' experience, good preaching skills, a deep faith, and a sense of humor." They do not seek a comedian who knows a lot of jokes. What they want is somebody who enjoys the Christian life, somebody who enjoys other people, and particularly, somebody who enjoys God.

From the other side of the pulpit, let me say this is what pastors also want. There is something life-giving about people who enjoy their faith. We want to be around people like that. Not only are they positive and affirming, but take delight in their faith. Joy is contagious, and most of us would love to be infected. Anne Lamott is right when she said, "Laughter is carbonated holiness."[18]

18 Anne Lamott, *Plan B: Further Thoughts on Faith* (New York: Penguin Books, 2006)

Consumed By Joy

I think of the teacher who enjoyed the Bible. Not only did she read it and study it, but she enjoyed it. Somebody asked, "What about the tough parts?" She said, "Oh, working through some of them is one reason why it's so fun." She loved to read the Bible, and it was infectious. People wanted to study the Bible with her.

Or there was Ken, who used to teach about generosity and giving as Christian disciplines. He said, "A tithe is only the beginning. When you give away fifteen or sixteen percent of your income, that is when it gets to be fun." We were visiting a worship service one time and the offering plates came around. Ken pulled out his wallet and unloaded it into the plate. He spontaneously gave about a dozen twenty-dollar bills. I whispered, "What are you doing? The sermon wasn't that good."

He giggled and said, "Wait!" I thought he was talking to me, but he was talking to the usher. Ken dug down into his left pocket and pulled out a wrinkled twenty-dollar bill, and said, "I forgot about that one." Then he laughed out loud — it was such a joyful laugh! He embodied in his generosity what the apostle Paul once wrote in a fund raising letter: "God loves a hilarious giver."[19] His generosity was contagious and I wanted to be around him.

What about Phoebe? She is a minister in a large city. She was showing me around the agency where she worked and her congregation started arriving. Some were homeless mothers, others were troubled by drugs, and many had a hard time taking care of themselves. Her job was to look every one of them in the eye and pray for them. If they needed anything else — a job reference, a ride to the medical clinic — she did what she could. Mostly she let them know that they were part of God's family. Because of her hair color, they called her Reverend Red.

One woman knocked on the office door and said, "I made you something, Reverend Red." The lady handed over a hat, stitched

19 2 Corinthians 9:7.

The Pilgrim Road

together from the pieces of a soda can with bright orange yarn. "Try it on, Reverend Red — that yarn is just like your hair." She laughed. Phoebe laughed, then put on the hat and wore it for the rest of the day. It was overwhelming to see so much freedom, so much joy. Whoever said working with the homeless is grim, difficult work?

Those on the Pilgrim Road know about joy. Joy is what finds us, what fills us, what keeps us in step with Jesus. We keep at the Christian life, not because we are always happy, but because there is a deeper quality of life in being about God's business and doing God's work.

Even Jesus himself — he knew about joy. Many people think he was serious all the time, but that was not the case. When he told all of his crazy parables, I think he winked when somebody nearby did not get the punch line. Clearly Jesus enjoyed his work because he kept doing it. It never seemed to wear him down when he spent a whole day around the hungry and the sick; he kept at it. When he faced resistance, opposition, and certain death, he persevered.

At least one New Testament writer understood the reason why. It is the anonymous writer of the letter to the Hebrews. He spent all of chapter eleven talking about the great people of faith. And then he began chapter twelve by saying, "Let us look to Jesus, the pioneer and perfecter of our faith, who for the sake of the joy that was set before him, endured the cross."[20]

To paraphrase it, why did Jesus go to the cross? Because of the joy, not just on the other side of the cross, but right in the middle of doing God's work.

Those who travel the road of discipleship know about this deep joy. There is a different quality of life when your life resonates with the love at the heart of the universe. There is a

20 Hebrews 12:2.

Consumed By Joy

higher level of understanding when you glimpse God's purposes for the world. There is a deeper capacity for patience when you discover how patient God is with all of us.

Most of all, there is great delight in knowing that God enjoys all who are faithful. In the words of another psalm, "God brought me out into a broad place; God delivered me, because he delighted in me."[21]

The pilgrim road is a hard but joyful road. The true spiritual journey weans us from all the false promises of the world and replaces them with the promises of God. Old burdens are lifted from our shoulders. Often they are replaced with new burdens from the hand of God. Yet those who know God's restoring power are never weighed down. If anything, they seem to keep shouting with joy.

21 Psalm 18:19.

Reflection Questions

"Consumed By Joy," Psalm 126

— How is joy different from happiness?

— Can I describe somebody who is joyful even though their life is hard?

— The psalm speaks of restoration and of God giving back something that was taken away. Can I tell any stories of where and how I have seen something restored?

— How is a sense of humor the sign of grace?

— Jewish humor often draws on the inconsistencies and paradoxes of everyday life. When have I laughed at something that didn't fit?

— When was the last time I had a really good belly laugh?

— Can I describe the people around me as joyful? Or are they "sour-faced saints"?

Eating Anxious Bread

A Song Of Ascents Of Solomon

*Unless the LORD builds the house, those who build it labor in
vain.*
Unless the LORD guards the city, the guard keeps watch in vain.
It is in vain that you rise up early and go late to rest,
eating the bread of anxious toil; for he gives sleep to his beloved.
*Sons are indeed a heritage from the LORD, the fruit of the womb a
reward.*
Like arrows in the hand of a warrior are the sons of one's youth.
Happy is the man who has his quiver full of them.
*He shall not be put to shame when he speaks with his enemies in
the gate.*   (Psalm 127: 1-5)

One summer I traveled into a canyon of red rocks in northern
New Mexico. It took two days to get there and the last hour was
on an impossibly rugged road. There were ditches and washouts
along the way. Clearly the people who lived at the end of the dirt
road wanted to be left alone. As I came around the final bend
before the dead end, I saw the Monastery of Christ in the Desert.
The adobe chapel sat beyond the banks of solar energy panels.
After I settled into the guest house, a bell called us to the final
worship service of the day.

Twenty monks in black robes quietly shuffled into the
sanctuary, each one bowing to the altar before sitting down. We
chanted the psalms for about a half hour, and this is the one I
remember: "Unless the Lord builds the house, those who build it
labor in vain."

As we stood to depart, the guestmaster scrambled over to
whisper hello. Two of us were new that night. Brother Andre

75

pointed us to the dining area, where the other half-dozen guests were headed. He whispered, "Do you have any questions?" I asked if it was true that the first worship service of each morning began at 4:00 a.m. He assured me that it did.

The other new guest, a young woman, asked the same question that my friends and family had asked repeatedly before I traveled to get there. "What is it, exactly, that you do in a monastery?" The guestmaster stopped abruptly, looked in shock, and said, "We do the work of God, of course." She did not ask what that meant.

Over the course of the next six days, his reply was embodied by our routine. The brothers in the monastery worship seven times each day, each service ranging from fifteen minutes to an hour and a half. There were periods for reading and study. Guests were expected to work a minimum of four hours each day, participating in the community tasks by scrubbing floors, weeding the garden, painting walls, or assisting in the kitchen.

As the guests spent a bit of time reflecting on their lives in the silence of the canyon, I noticed that each monk had tasks assigned to their skills. A few were mechanics, and others made sandals and robes. There were beekeepers and website designers, cooks and scholars, and at least three brothers who lived in private huts to do nothing less than pray all day and night.

With a two hour time-zone change from my travels, the 3:45 morning wake-up bell wasn't so bad. The routine of seven worship services was a wonderful framework for our day. The manual labor was reasonable and necessary, especially for the climate. One day I painted linseed oil on wooden posts parched by the high desert air.

It was not all work and no play. On the Feast Day of St. Benedict, the abbot announced a volleyball game and a chicken barbecue. When one of the brothers was ordained as a Roman Catholic deacon at the end of the week, there was a feast of

Eating Anxious Bread

Vietnamese food with more wine than anybody has ever seen outside of a fraternity party.

This was "the work of God." The Latin phrase is *Opus Dei*. As Saint Benedict first explained it, our human work is to pray, specifically to pray all the psalms in a given week, and to function together as a community.

What do people do in a monastery? Pretty much whatever they do *outside* a monastery, except that there are some key differences. There is, of course, the foundation of praying the psalms. The day is drenched in scripture, so there is always some text for meditation. Apart from that obvious difference for most people, there were two major differences: balance and overlap.

First, there was balance to each day. There was a time for work, a time for reflection, a time for play, and a time for rest. No task or chore dominated over the others. Scrubbing the toilet was as important to the community as reflecting on the scriptures. Meals were not rushed. Nobody stayed up late, for the morning bell would always ring, ready or not.

Second, the work of God is human work. The brothers aspired to have a complete overlap between what God wants to accomplish in the world and what people are called to do. There are no wasted pursuits or aimless tasks. Nobody asks, "What does this matter?" The work we do is the work that God makes possible and wishes to have done. Because our day is balanced, we are free to enjoy our work as a gift.

The eighth Psalm of Ascent, Psalm 127, offers a reflection on our daily work. As we travel the pilgrim road, the psalmist warns us to keep a balance between what we do and what God does. Recall how the psalmist begins:

Unless the Lord builds the house, those who build it labor in vain.
Unless the Lord guards the city, the guard keeps watch in vain.
It is in vain that that you rise up early and late to rest, eating the

bread of anxious toil,
for the Lord gives sleep to his beloved.

In vain, in vain, in vain — three times the psalmist hammers that phrase. He knows how we can spend a lot of our days in empty effort. Maybe we are employed to do things that do not really matter to the wider world. Or we fritter away our spare time on cell phone calls and solitaire games on the computer. It is possible to live a full day and have absolutely nothing to show for it. It is also possible to die without ever having lived — *in vain, in vain, in vain.*

What we do with each day matters. It matters that we work, play, and rest. We work, in the hope that our work will overlap with God's work. We play, so that we can enjoy our relationships and the natural world that God has birthed us into. We rest because we are not infinite and God, who is infinite, can work while we sleep.

How often do we "eat the bread of anxious toil?" I love that tasty metaphor. It reminds us that anxiety is not a new disorder. The psalmist knew we can become so insulated from God that we think we are paying our own way through the planet, eating only what we produce from our own effort. So we hover. We get pushy. We insist that things turn out our way. Pretty soon we are grinding our teeth while we sleep, worrying whether or not we have enough resources to survive until we die. You know what the psalmist has to say about that? — *in vain, in vain, in vain.*

Few of us are called to a life in a monastery. We don't have a rigid schedule that determines when we work, play, or sleep. Pretty much, we are on our own, and we appreciate the freedom.

But in our freedom, we often fall back into another kind of slavery. Ask somebody, "How are you doing?" The number one response that I hear is "I'm busy." It does not matter if it

Eating Anxious Bread

is the business executive or the retired grandparent. People will say the same thing when they are on vacation or when they lie in a hospital bed: "I'm busy." Lots of people brag about their busyness, wearing their busyness as a badge of honor, as if it is a blessing to be worn out from doing so much. As someone writes,

Busyness has become a way of life for many of us, even a status symbol. Our work is justified only if we are continually active and preoccupied. There are so many necessary and urgent things to be done. After one task is completed, there are others always waiting in the wings, needing our immediate attention. To slow down, to rest, often seems out of the question, a lack of commitment, a sign of weakness. Not only our days but many of our evenings and weekends become billed, too. We are not just eating this bread of anxious toil; we are daily gulping down loaf after loaf.[22]

So the psalmist gives the warning: "Unless the Lord builds the house, those who build it labor in vain." God cannot do any work if we are doing all the work. If there is nothing but ceaseless activity on our part, we are led in our vanity to think that life is up to us.

To illustrate, the psalmist reminds us of the serious business of making children. Have you ever made a child? Of all the work God gave to the human race, it is actually kind of fun. In fact, we may know some people who enjoyed such work, only to later discover that a child had been made. Stop and think about this for a second. Creating a new person is our work, but it is really God's work. Child-making is an occasion where human work and divine work coincide. Father and mother offer something of themselves, but it is God who creates human life.

Perhaps the worst thing we can do, from cradle to grave, is to boast about how busy we are. If I might add a pastoral word,

22 Joe Roos, "Eating the Bread of Anxious Toil," Wide Quaker Fellowship Publications, Fall 2006. http://fwccamericas.org/publications/wqf/2006_fall/breadoftoil.shtml

we simply are not that important. We are not the center of the universe, and we do not succeed in life on our own strength. "Unless the Lord builds the house, those who build it labor in vain."

Perhaps that is, right here in the middle of a song about work, the psalmist speaks of sleep. God "gives sleep to his beloved." It is a holy gift. We are designed in such a way that we must be recharged. Did you ever stop to remember that a third of our lives are spent in sleep? Did you think that there's something holy about snoring? The other people in your bed might not think so, but it is true. It is possible to burn the candle at both ends, said the psalmist. We can rise early and lie down late for the best of intentions. But if that is all we do, pretty soon we find ourselves chewing on the "bread of anxious toil." Our jaws will begin to hurt.

By contrast, sleep is God's gift. According to the psalmist, sleep is given to God's beloved. That would include all of us, whoever, wherever we are. We cannot keep working if we are drifting off to sleep. That is all right for, as one of the previous psalms tells us, the Lord of Israel neither slumbers nor sleeps. The Lord will keep us, guard us. The Lord will build what we cannot.

Sadly, there are plenty of people who pay this lip service and proceed to burn themselves out. Religious people seem particularly prone to this distortion. We can name obsessive pastors and frantic church volunteers. They push themselves to hover over matters as if they are ruling heaven and earth. In one of his books, Eugene Peterson gives this malady an ancient Latin name, *Irreligiosa sollicitudo pro Deo*, which he defined as a "blasphemous anxiety to do God's work for him."[23] Peterson

23 Eugene Peterson, *The Contemplative Pastor* (Grand Rapids: William B. Eerdmans Publishing, 1993) 18-19.

asked the probing question: All this busyness in my life, am I really that indispensable and important? Or have I somehow chosen to be this busy, not wanting to notice that I had a choice in the matter, but working hard because I guess I should be? According to Peterson, we are busy for one of two reasons: either we are busy because we are vain or because we are lazy.

The most severe case in my memory was a minister of a church in a town where I once lived. He often boasted of how he had built the congregation to twelve hundred members, without the help of other clergy staff members. Those were the good old days, to be sure, but one could detect some obsession in his story. While his wife lay dying in a hospital bed one Christmas Eve, he insisted on preaching at all three worship services, a decision that his grown daughters never forgave. His wife died and he was nowhere in sight. After he retired, his church gave him a house around the block, where he could see inside the church office from his kitchen window. He continued to accept invitations to baptize, wed, and bury, much to the chagrin of his successors. In time, the church declined, partially due to its beloved former pastor's inability to rest. There is a kind of sloth where people work so hard that they cease to trust in God.

What did the psalmist warn? "Unless the Lord builds the house, those who build it labor in vain."

Some time ago I found myself on the Isle of Lewis. It is a peat-covered rock, some thirty miles off the western shore of Scotland. Lewis is an austere landscape, windy enough that few trees can grow there. The air is starkly Presbyterian. On the sabbath, the whole island shuts down. Nothing moves unless it is going to church. People worship. They nap. They walk with their spouses. They enjoy their children. They keep the computers off and pretty much ignore their televisions.

I asked a parish minister about the practice. With a thick brogue he told the truth. "Keeping the sabbath is a good preparation for our deaths. We cease from our labors so God can fill in the gaps. We rest so God can finish what we cannot." Some may be offended by such bluntness, but it seemed a remarkable telling of the truth. It also is a refreshing way to embrace the work and rhythm of our lives. Life is not primarily about us and what we accomplish; it's really about a God who holds everything together even while we are resting.

"Unless the Lord builds the house…" The Lord cannot build anything if we have pushed God out of the picture. But in weekly sabbath and evening sleep, God can do his restorative work within us.

When we wake and return to our plows, we pray that everything we do might be the work of God.

Eating Anxious Bread

Reflection Questions

"Eating Anxious Bread," Psalm 127

— Reflect on the past day. How much work did I do — and how much work did God do within me?

— Can I name three unnecessary things that I have done since dawn?

— Is it difficult for me to rest from my labor?

— What are the significant time-wasters in my life? What would it take to eliminate them?

— When was the last time I complained about being "too busy"? Was I?

— How is our ability to sleep an indicator of the condition of our souls?

— What did God accomplish in the world while I slept last night?

The Happiness Of Fear

A Song Of Ascents

Happy is everyone who fears the LORD, who walks in his ways.
You shall eat the fruit of the labor of your hands;
you shall be happy, and it shall go well with you.
Your wife will be like a fruitful vine within your house;
your children will be like olive shoots around your table.
Thus shall the man be blessed who fears the LORD.
The LORD bless you from Zion.
May you see the prosperity of Jerusalem all the days of your life.
May you see your children's children. Peace be upon Israel!

(Psalm 128: 1-6)

At first hearing, this sounds like the ideal psalm for a traditional Father's Day. Clearly it is written from a guy's point of view. With tongue in cheek, I have tried to imagine it as the screenplay for an off-kilter religious commercial.

Zoom in to catch a contented man sitting in an overstuffed recliner. His legs are propped up. There is a ball game on the flat screen television, and he is opening the mail. Bring the camera in to look over his shoulder. It is a statement from his brokerage account, and we see the close-up of a whopping bottom line. Cut to a quick shot of the smile on his face. Yes, he shall enjoy the fruit of his labor.

The second camera pulls back, and we see his wife entering the room. She is wearing an apron and her blond hair bounces on the top of her shoulders. What's that in her hands? It is a tray with a large frosted mug of an amber beverage and three different bowls of pretzels, chips, and double-stuff Oreos. Obviously our man of the hour has married well. His wife is like a fruitful vine

84

around the house — and her passionate kiss starts him thinking about the halftime show. She pulls away to get a warm apple pie out of the oven.

Just then — what's that movement to his left, at the window? Why, it's his three obedient children: Buck Junior, Robbie, and little Christina. Oh, they are so full of smiles as they look in upon his reverie! Junior taps on the window and said, "Dad, we're done picking up all the trash around the yard. You can practice some shots on your sand wedge whenever you are ready." The sheer joy of having children like that! They are like olive shoots, so full of life, hope, and promise.

We see our hero smile. Here is a joyful man without a care in the world. So the honey-voiced announcer recites the words now appearing on the screen: "Happy is everyone who fears the Lord, who walks in God's ways" (Psalm 128).

Men, isn't this how Father's Day looks at your house? Like some kind of dream ... until somebody slaps you and says, "Wake up!" Even in the "perfect home," this is not how it goes. Not for one day, much less the other 364 days of the year.

We have to remember that the psalmist was trying to describe pictures of the ideal life in his own day, probably from some 2,400 years ago. For better or worse, ancient Israel was a man's world. In that time and culture, an adult male was considered cursed if he was not married, and deprived if he did not have children. And, if he was married and had some children, he was considered blessed by God. A wife and children were seen as examples of a greater heavenly benevolence. God loved you, so God blessed you with such gifts.

So, we need to scratch beneath the surface here. The issue is not "marriage" and "children." The issue is the blessing of God, and the extent to which that blessing is related to our faithfulness. The first verse of the ninth Song of Ascent tosses the issue into the air as a beatitude: "Happy is everyone who fears the Lord, who walks in God's ways."

This is a universal declaration, and that alone should make us a little suspicious. The psalmist said, "Happy is everyone..." Really? Everyone? Are we to believe that such happiness is automatic? Is there a direct relationship between what we do and what we receive? I can name a dozen people who are walking in God's ways, living and loving as Christ lives and loves, but it is not going well for them. There may be trouble at home, sickness in their bones, or even the dread of an upcoming birthday. Sometimes people do the right thing and they hit the wall...or the wall hits them. Happiness is not an automatic benefit of the Christian life. Last we checked, Jesus wasn't particularly cheerful when he was beaten and nailed on the cross.

Truth be told, that is not what the psalmist is saying anyway. The emphasis is not on the happiness, or even on its evidence. The gravitational center of the psalm, mentioned twice, is "the fear of the Lord." The happy person is the one who fears God. The blessed one is the one who fears the Lord.

We need to take a few minutes to wrestle with a definition. What does it mean to fear the Lord?

As you may recall, this is a popular phrase in the Bible. It comes up hundreds and hundreds of times. Here are a few samplings:

- The fear of the Lord is the beginning of wisdom (Proverbs 1:7).

- The fear of the Lord is the fountain of life (Proverbs 14:27).

- Happy are those who fear the Lord (Psalm 112:1).

The Happiness Of Fear

- Fear the Lord your God (and) love God and keep the commandments for your own well-being (Deuteronomy 10:12-13).

It was said of the Messiah, "His delight shall be in the fear of the Lord."[24] One ancient text from the book of Genesis declares that one of God's names is *The Fear*.[25]

Over and over again the Bible says, "Fear God." Or to be proper about it, "Fear the Lord your God." According to books like Deuteronomy, Moses said the heart of true faith is to fear the Lord your God.

Sometimes we use other words to say the same thing. In scripture, the word "fear" is often translated "worship," as in "worship the Lord your God." The original Hebrew word is also translated as "having a feeling of awe, amazement, or wonder," as if to say a true glimpse of God gives you a sense of God's size, power, and majesty.

More often, though, to fear God means to respect God, to affirm the great distance that lies between God's ways and our own. In the words of Walter Zimmerli, "The fear of God means walking under a heaven that is mysteriously closed, walking without the assurance that lightning might not suddenly shoot out and strike you as you go — at every step relying upon the free gift of God, but at every step also summoned to suffer the riddle and oppression that God can inflict."[26] We never know what will happen on any given day. It might be good, it might not, but either way, say the scriptures, "blessed be the Lord." This is how it is to fear God.

Let me suggest there are benefits to a reverence of heart

24 Isaiah 11:3.
25 Genesis 31:42
26 Quoted in Roland E. Murphy, *The Tree of Life: An Exploration of Biblical Wisdom Literature* (Grand Rapids: William B. Eerdmans Publishing, 2002) 56.

and mind. Holy fear does at least three things: 1) it limits our importance, 2) it deepens our trust, and 3) it awakens us to gifts.

First, if we fear God, it puts a limit on our importance. It removes us from the center of all things. God is greater than us. God understands what we do not. God will save what we cannot. God can finish what we will not.

There are few more truthful words in a high-achievement culture like ours. They slice through our illusions of control and expertise. They remind us of how little we can actually manage or manipulate. This is a hard truth, but ultimately a healthy one. To say it in the words of another psalm, "It is God who made us and not we ourselves."[27]

We have a hundred ways to dismiss this truth. There is a self-made man of my acquaintance. Through sheer aggression and drive, he has pushed his career to the top of the heap, and received great financial rewards. He dines well, thanks to his high salary, and thinks nothing of claiming it as the fruit of hard work.

His third wife is indeed a fruitful vine, the mother of his children, although the previous two were abruptly discarded. The first wife was his college sweetheart, who worked two jobs to put him through graduate school. Three months into his executive job, he had an affair with a co-worker with the same education, so each divorced and married one another. "She seemed more my type," he said. Indeed she was: the career came first for each of them. When the company transferred her three states away, he refused to relocate, which explains divorce number two.

Pushing forty, still climbing the ladder, without any family ties, he began to date a young waitress at his country club. When she announced their first child was on the way, they scheduled a glorious wedding on a beach in the Dominican Republic. Two more children later, they now live in a cul-de-sac in an expensive

27 Psalm 100:3.

neighborhood. They don't go to church frequently. He says, "I don't go in for all that guilt and God stuff."

A psalm like this can be a reminder of all the wreckage such a person has created by enthroning himself as the supreme authority on his own life. He is accountable to no one but himself. He pops anti-depressants when nobody is looking and washes them down with a little too much scotch.

It reminds me of the old joke. How many narcissists does it take to change a light bulb? Answer: only one. He holds the light bulb in the air and the world revolves around him.

To fear God is to get ourselves out of the way, to move ourselves out of the middle, to let God be God. To paraphrase Jesus, the best way to move ahead is by putting ourselves last. God-fearing people live with humility and keep a sense of their own limits. They cannot do everything or be everywhere. The better challenge is to do something and to be somewhere, and then to leave everything else up to the ruler of the universe.

Second, if we can keep that straight, then we have the opportunity to trust God more deeply. If we affirm that we cannot do everything, then the remainder of what we cannot do is in the hands of the one who can do even more. If life's challenges are greater than our ability to meet them, then we can put them into the hands of a God who first placed each star in the sky. And they will be in good hands.

As Karl Barth said in one of his writings, "We must fear God above all things because we love him above all things."[28] God is the only one who is worthy of our honor, our obedience, and our love. Barth said, "When we love God above all things, we are never disappointed."

Every day of our lives, we come across something that can

28 Karl Barth, *Church Dogmatics, Vol. 2: The Doctrine of God* (Edinboro: T. &T. Clark, 1957), 33.

make us afraid. We can fear the loss of our health, loved ones, money, jobs, reputations, and dreams. If we are honest, we know that sooner or later we will lose all of them anyway. We are afraid that we might lose them today and that everything will no longer be under our control. The only thing that can trump the fears of life is a better kind of fear — the reverence and respect for the God who keeps rescuing his people and saving the world.

One thing to remember about the fear of God is that sooner or later, it comes for all of us. Sooner or later we will go up against some situation we cannot fix. There will be a moment when we are helpless, weak, and incapable. Everybody gets a turn at this. It simply comes.

It is good to rehearse this before it happens. Here is what we have to decide: will we throw ourselves into God's arms? Will we vainly try to fix everything? Or will we stand back and whine about our situation? The only way through is by choosing between two different kinds of fear: We can fear the world or we can fear the Lord. Knowing the difference is the beginning of wisdom.

We trust God, fear God, and love God. The impulse behind each verb is the same. Either we do not trust, fear, and love — or we do. That is our daily decision and we have a lot of practice. When we jump wholeheartedly toward God, we trust we will be caught. But we will never know this for sure until we jump.

That brings us to the third benefit of fearing the Lord. Not only is it an opportunity to learn the limit to our importance, not only does it deepen our trust in God, but we claim a new awakening to see everything as a gift. Everything is a gift. So perhaps the old psalmist is wiser than we might have thought.

Those of us who have children know they are a gift. We did not earn them or even work for them. They were given to us, even if they weren't expected. Like a sixty-year-old friend said when he and his wife were expecting a child that was not medically possible: "The Lord giveth and we shall hereby nickname our son 'Oops,' which is Swedish for 'gift from God.'"

Or as John Calvin says in his commentary on this psalm, a good spouse is a gift. Fortunately, he did not decree for all time and culture what makes for a good spouse — but those of us who have had the benefit of a loving companion know exactly what he is talking about. She or he is a blessing, a gift, a sign that God provides when God chooses to provide. We cannot force a gift; we receive a gift. And the gifts keep coming all the time.

To see our children's children, to take delight in the work we do, to touch the future, to enjoy the present; these are some of the many signs that God loves us. Undoubtedly, we can think of a few more.

According to the theme of Psalm 128, true happiness begins with a life-giving kind of fear. As we live with a healthy reverence for the God who loves us, pretty soon we begin to see God's blessings in a new and deeper way. We move from thinking that it is all up to us, to trusting that all gifts come from the hand of the Lord.

We are the blessed ones, you and I. God wants us to be happy, to enjoy life's journey, and desires that all things should turn out well. These gifts and blessings do not come automatically or anonymously. But they do come all the time.

God's promise comes with them, in the words of the apostle Paul: *"All things work together for good for those who love God, who are called according to his purpose."*[29]

---

29 Romans 8:28

Reflection Questions

"The Happiness Of Fear," Psalm 128

— What does the phrase "fear of God" mean to me?

— Am I afraid of God? How is that different from honoring God?

— How would I describe the perfect life? In my time and culture, what are the signs of God's blessing?

— Can I name some ways that my self-importance has been punctured?

— How easy is it for me to trust God with my life?

— How are the people in my household a gift from God?

— What are some ways that I put God's intentions ahead of my own?

Known By Their Limp

A Song Of Ascents

"Often have they attacked me from my youth" — let Israel now say —
"often have they attacked me from my youth, yet they have not prevailed against me.
The plowers plowed on my back; they made their furrows long."
The LORD is righteous; he has cut the cords of the wicked.
May all who hate Zion be put to shame and turned backward.
Let them be like the grass on the housetops that withers before it grows up,
with which reapers do not fill their hands or binders of sheaves their arms,
while those who pass by do not say, "The blessing of the LORD be upon you!
We bless you in the name of the LORD!" (Psalm 129: 1-8)

Along the pilgrim road, we must take the time to regard our enemies. Enemies — it is not only that there are natural difficulties, physical challenges, and spiritual distractions on our journey, there are people out there who wish us ill. The psalmist took time to begin working this through.

One way to do it is through revenge. Maybe you have heard the old Irish prayer, which I first heard from a priest named McGowan. He was called upon to offer a blessing, and this is what he said:

May those who love us, love us,
and those who do not love us, may God turn their hearts,
and if God cannot turn their hearts, may he turn their ankles
that we may know them by their limping.

The Pilgrim Road

We laughed when he told it at the Rubber Chicken banquet. It seemed so Irish: the joyfulness, the turn of the phrase, the little twist of judgment that would seem so delightful ("that we may know them by their limping"). We laughed, because it seemed so funny. It was vindictive, but funny.

In the Bible's prayer book, we have a psalm that sounds like this. Psalm 129 is a prayer for the downfall of Israel's enemies. The psalmist stops in his tracks, shakes his fist in the air, and hurls a curse: "May all who hate Zion be put to shame and turned backward!" Or to put it another way, 'Lord, give them a little limp!'

Notice, if you will, that the psalmist did not use ink in scripture to call down judgment on his personal enemies — say, on the butcher who cheated him or the neighbor who dumped dirty dishwater on the lawn. Rather, this is righteous anger. He was angry with God's enemies, the ones who "hated Zion," the ones who disrespected the ways and the worship of God. He prayed that their hatred would cause public shame to heap on their heads. He wanted those who despise God's presence on the earth to be exposed and embarrassed.

But he could not keep it there, so he offered another little curse. Apparently the psalmist looked around the countryside and his imagination began to flutter. He saw the peasant housing with the rooftops made from sod. What's more, it must have been another hot day in Palestine, for he said,

Let them be like the grass on the housetops that withers before it grows up,
Let them be like the grass which reapers can't use or share with the farm animal.
Let them be like the ones who will not hear the blessing of the Lord.

In other words, "So there, you dried-up rooftops!" That doesn't translate really well, but perhaps we hear the gist of it.

Known By Their Limp

We have all heard, or uttered, more afflictive curses. For instance, there is the curse uttered by a Jewish rabbi: "May all of your teeth fall out, except for the one tooth that gives you a toothache." Or there is the response of the Palestinian shepherd: "May the fleas of a thousand camels infest your armpits!" Somehow when the psalmist cursed, "May you become like dried grass on a rooftop," it does not quite cut it. But we understand the sentiment.

A man that I know recently wrote me an email from another state. It seems his home life had been a wreck as of late. Kevin had a young daughter, about six years old, and he never got to see her. His ex-wife had primary custody of the girl, and she moved away with her without saying a word. She left no address, no phone number, and that was not their agreement.

He tracked them down through a private detective. Upon getting the address, he appeared on the doorstep. The mother slammed the door and called the police, accusing Kevin of stalking them. While two police officers showed up to discuss the matter with him, he could hear his little girl screaming on the other side of the wall. She had caught a glimpse of her daddy and she missed him. The situation went downhill from there.

I do not know the whole story, and it is not really my business anyway. Suffice it to say, after numerous court hearings, considerable pain, and great expense, Kevin had been asking for prayers. He confessed that he did not know what to pray for, so he prayed God would smite the people who brought his daughter pain. He has special scorn for a child therapist who lied on the witness stand and then later was tripped up by her lies.

"Pray for me," he said, "but pray for my daughter. It is awful that we can spend together only two hours a month, supervised by a representative of the court. The whole situation is really difficult on her. She has begun to punch other children in her school and has tantrums for no apparent reason."

The Pilgrim Road

We know these stories. Some people among us know them painfully well. Wishing for fleas or turned ankles are mild punishments compared to some of the dark curses that can invade the heart. People are capable of doing horrendous things to one another. Then they perpetuate the warfare. I hear weariness when the psalmist says, 'Often they have attacked me from my youth ...they have taken a farm plow and run it across my back so that the furrows are deep.'

I have known people who love to pick a fight, just because they are not comfortable to live in peace. When things go too quietly, they share a gossiping word, speak the innuendo, or play people off one another like pawns in a chess game. Sometimes they do it because they are bored, or because they are cruel. Once in a while, the motivation is that they cannot live with peace and quiet.

In other situations, it can be a sense of justice that stirs the pot. For some people, it is the feeling that fairness would not be fair. A woman was recently arrested for setting her own home on fire. She explained by saying, "The judge told me that I had to sell the house and share the profits with my estranged husband, but I could not bear to have him end up with so much." Well, guess what — she received her wish. These days, she also has a lot of time to think about what she did.

In spite of each situation and its bag of tangled truths, the one thing we can say about our enemies is that they can be enormous distractions from the pilgrim road. Enemies tie up our courtrooms and tangle up our hearts. They provoke us, sometimes without our conscious awareness. They prompt us to consider violence. And it is not only our enemies who consume us — sometimes the very ways we respond to them will consume us.

As Frederick Buechner once described the unsavory truth,

Known By Their Limp

Of the Seven Deadly Sins, anger is possibly the most fun. To lick your wounds, to smack your lips over grievances long past, to roll over your tongue the prospect of bitter confrontations still to come, to savor to the last toothsome morsel both the pain you are given and the pain you are giving back — in many ways it is a feast fit for a king. The chief drawback is that what you are wolfing down is yourself. The skeleton at the feast is you.[30]

We laughed when the Irish priest prayed for God to twist the ankles of our enemies. But some of that laughter was nervous. It is simply not healthy to live by revenge. Revenge has uncertain benefits. As Mahatma Gandhi is reported to have said, "If you live by the rule of an eye for an eye, pretty soon the whole world is blind." Somehow the animosity must cease. We have to let it go.

In the center of the psalm is the important affirmation: "The Lord is righteous." God sees things without the scalding tears of hostility. God is the judge who can make things right. God is the one who stands outside the circle of our disputes. God is concerned but immovable; loving, but unable to be bribed.

God's righteousness is clearly revealed when the world crucifies his own son, and neither one of them retaliates in revenge. Instead we hear our Jesus say, "Father, forgive them, they don't know what they are doing." Our hope is that God has answered that prayer, that God continues to answer that prayer, for the Lord alone is righteous. Forgiveness is the way of God with infinite mercy. Frustrating as it might possibly be, God inevitably sets everything right.

There is a sadly comical scene in the biblical short story of Jonah. As you may remember, Jonah is a reluctant prophet. When sent to preach doom and gloom to the nasty people of Nineveh,

---

30 Frederick Buechner, *Wishful Thinking: A Theological ABC* (New York: Harper & Row, Publishers, 1973), 2.

he hopped a ship to go in the other direction. God used a storm and big fish to return Jonah to shore and redirected him to his commission. Bleached white by the gastric juices of the fish's stomach, the prophet hobbled his way to Nineveh, preached his fiery sermon, and waited for God to blast away his enemies.

However, the people of Nineveh changed their minds, and that changed God's mind. The moment of judgment never comes. Jonah was furious. As the poet Thomas John Carlisle voiced the prophet's fury, "I hate God's enemies with a perfect hatred; why can't God do likewise?"[31]

The best answer: because this is not the kind of God that we have. God did not condemn the world for killing Jesus, deciding instead to transform the world through the power of forgiveness.

Ever so quietly, the psalmist remembers that we are not defined by our enemies, but by the covenant love of God. We have felt the plow cutting on our backs, but our enemies have not had the last word. "God has cut the bonds of the wicked," so we are no longer tied down, tied up, or twisted into knots. It is possible to be cut free. Let the angry burden go. You have carried it long enough. Let it go. Let God set you free.

Some years ago, my church had a congregational memorial service on a Sunday afternoon in March. It was the first time we had ever tried that service, and I am glad that it has now become a regular practice for our congregation sometime each Lent. Here is what we do. After the sermon and a hymn, we invite people forward to light a candle on the communion table and speak a name. They say the name of somebody who has passed away, somebody for whom they still mourn. It might be a tearful moment, but it can also be a moment of healing and affirmation. Following that recital of names, we gather together and enjoy a

31 Thomas John Carlisle, *You! Jonah!* (Grand Rapids: Wm. B. Eerdmans Publishing Co. 1968), 43.

meal.

A young woman named Helen attended with her husband and three children. They came forward and lit a candle as a family. Her husband had recently lost his mother, so he spoke her name, paused for a moment of silence, wiped away a few tears, and they returned to their seat.

A few minutes later, Helen came back, this time by herself. She lit another candle, and said another name. It was a name I had never heard, loud and clear, and I wouldn't have thought anything of it except for the strange look that was on her face.

The memorial service came to an end, and everybody scattered. A few hours later, I received an e-mail from Helen. "I surprised myself," she said. "I never thought I could say that name. I don't know where this is going. Could we get together and talk?"

We sat in my study the next morning and the story came tumbling out. It had been her brother, she said. He had been dead for sixteen years, and this was the first time she allowed herself to speak his name. The two of them had been the children of a minister and her brother Eric had a full-blown rebellion as a teenager. "To say that he and my father didn't get along would be a gross understatement," she said. Their relationship grew violent. They threatened to actively do harm to one another.

The situation became so bad that Eric sat down and wrote a letter. He renounced the father and everything he stood for, cursed him for this reason and that, and then went to his bedroom and took his own life. The final insult was that he did it on a Good Friday, while his father was leading a worship service at a nearby church.

Well, the father was not to be outdone. He refused to print an obituary. He refused to allow a funeral for his son. He arranged for a quick cremation, and told the mother and sister that they would scatter the ashes later at their summer home in the mountains. Then the father decreed that the name of his son would never again be spoken in his home.

Sixteen years later, Helen came down the aisle in our church. For the first time in years, she spoke her brother's name. "I don't know where this is going," she said, "but I need to put it to rest."

She said the one continuing reminder of her brother was his duffel bag. After he died, the parents cleaned out his room, wiping away every memory. They gave Helen his duffel bag. Not knowing what else to do with it, unable to throw it away, she carried that baggage with her for the next sixteen years.

Now it was time to let go of the burden. About a week later Helen, her husband, and I gathered at a country cemetery up in the mountains. Helen had a shoebox with a scoop or two of soil from the backyard where her brother's ashes had been scattered, the charred remains of that duffel bag which she decided to no longer carry, and a letter of reconciliation that she wrote to her brother. We laid those relics in the ground and gave her brother a proper funeral.

Sooner or later along the pilgrim toad, we have to put some things to rest. We have the power to lay our burdens down. We leave them in the hands of the God, who alone is righteous, a God in whose justice the whole world has its hope.

Reflection Questions

"Know By Their Limp," Psalm 129

— Can I name anybody who wishes me evil?

— Have I wished them the same?

— When was the last time that I insulted somebody?

— Is there some conflict in my life that remains unsettled?

— What tangible ways could I hand over that situation to God?

— Is there an ongoing situation that makes me angry? What can I do about it? What do I have to trust that God will do about it?

Out Of The Depths

A Song Of Ascents

Out of the depths I cry to you, O LORD.
Lord, hear my voice!
Let your ears be attentive to the voice of my supplications!
If you, O LORD, should mark iniquities, Lord, who could stand?
But there is forgiveness with you, so that you may be revered.
I wait for the LORD, my soul waits, and in his word I hope;
my soul waits for the Lord
more than those who watch for the morning,
more than those who watch for the morning.
O Israel, hope in the LORD!
For with the LORD there is steadfast love,
and with him is great power to redeem.
It is he who will redeem Israel from all its iniquities.

(Psalm 130: 1-8)

One of the mirages along the pilgrim road is that faith will flatten the highway. Every traveler knows there will be twists and turns on the journey. But some are lulled to believe the road to God is an easy trip. They want to believe the path is not too steep, and that is a lie.

In every generation, there are false prophets who sell empty promises. They claim, "If you say certain words, they will save you." If you will do specific things, your life will improve. Some of the most scurrilous of these scoundrels will draw a direct line from the good deeds that people do to the blessings they should expect from an appreciative God.

The pilgrim road is a hard road. It has some deep potholes. The psalm for today comes from somebody at the bottom of one of those potholes. "Out of the depths I cry to you, O Lord! Lord, hear my voice!" If the last stop along the road was Psalm 129 and the affliction of enemies outside of us, Psalm 130 surveys the tortured interior landscape of a human soul. 'I cry out of the depths,' lamented the psalmist. That is a nautical term from the sea. The water is over his head; He has nowhere to put down his feet.

There is a great joy in following Jesus. I have written of that before. But there is also great pain along the way, a good bit of it our own making. Psalm 130 assumes this. Like the rest of the psalms, it has no pretensions before God. From the depths, there is the cry of prayer, the assurance of forgiveness, and a good share of patient waiting. We are reminded of what we already know: that life is difficult and the journey will take some perseverance.

Some people avoid such psalms, calling them gloomy or oppressive. The truth, is many of us have honest friends whom we avoid because they are honest. They love us, so they tell it like it is. That can be more than we want to handle. So our pain stays untouched and therefore unhealed. It stays in our gut until we dare to face the truth about our hurts.

The writer Frederick Buechner was invited to speak to a group of church people in Texas. "Is there something you want me to address?" he asked. The conference leader said, "Tell us about a defining moment in your life. What was an event that made you who you are?"

Buechner thought about that question. Then he told them a story from early childhood, a story he had never told anybody. When he was growing up, there was a lot of alcohol in his home. It was the 1930s, during the Great Depression, and nobody had a lot of money. But there was a lot of drinking going on and it was an unsettling time for him as a child.

One night his father came back from somewhere. He had had

too much to drink. Fred's mother did not want the father to drive the car. Somehow she slipped the keys away from him, took them to her ten-year-old son, and said, "Don't let your father have these." The boy was already in bed. He took the car keys and held them in his fist under the pillow. His father seemed to know he had them. He came and said, "Give me the keys. I need them. I have to go out some place."

Fred was just a child. He was frightened. He didn't know what to say, and could not move. He lay there as his father pleaded, "Give me the keys." He pulled the covers over his head, trying to escape, finally falling asleep with his father's voice in his ears. Years later, the story was still with him, and it symbolized so much of what Fred had survived during his childhood, long before his father committed suicide a few years later.

The room was quiet as Fred finished telling his story. Then one of the conference leaders said something that Fred did not expect to hear. He said, "You have had a fair amount of pain in your life, like everybody else. You have been a good steward of it."[32]

Who could expect that kind of insight? "You have been a good steward of your pain. You have handled it well." It was never anything that Fred or anybody else would ever set out to do. With enough steps on the pilgrim road, however, personal pain is something that we have to handle. We might feel tempted to pull the covers over our heads, but there are moments that all of us remember: moments when the adults around us did not act responsibly, moments when we lost our innocence or cried ourselves to sleep. It is tempting to brush these memories off our shoulders. They are hard to handle. They are disturbing to remember.

But the way of the pilgrim road is to be good stewards of our

32 Frederick Buechner, *Telling Secrets* (New York: Harper Collins, 1991).

pain. So we cry to God "out of the depths." Too often we speak from the shallows. Or we surf along the top of the water. The psalm jumps into deeper water — because that is the only place where we can be healed.

Years ago, I went through a time when I felt emotionally unsettled. Like anybody else, I tried not to let it show, especially in church. Inside my soul, there were a lot of doubts and fears, and I was quickly reaching wit's end. A friend suggested that I visit a church that he had told me about. "It is an uplifting place," he said, "and you might find it helpful."

So, one free Sunday morning, I packed my knapsack full of worries and took it with me as I slipped into one of that church's pews. The sermon title was promising: "Dealing with Life's Temptations." The preacher got up and talked about his habit of jogging. He didn't know what to do, he said, because his jogging route took him right by a donut shop. He could smell the fresh donuts coming off the line. It was overpowering. So, he decided to jog along another road.

That was his sermon. That was all he said. I kept waiting for him to say something more, but he didn't. Instead he joked about his waistline and how his wife might be upset if he had a Boston Cream donut or two. Was this for real? I looked around the room, wondering if anybody else felt like me. Most folks looked glazed over — just like some of his donuts.

"Come on, pal," I quietly cheered. "Can't you show us that you live on the same street as the rest of us? Can't you plumb the depths of how it really feels to be tempted?" Unfortunately, he never went there. Instead he kept skipping stones on the top of ocean, never noticing that every one of those stones eventually sank. I left that church discouraged and feeling neglected.

Then on the way home, it hit me: how many times have I spoken superficially? Put on the rose-colored glasses and glided through another person's difficulty?

How many times have I done whatever possible to push away pain at arm's length, rather than to let it teach me something? Perhaps to teach me to deepen my sympathy and thicken my soul?

How many times have I splashed around in the shallow end of the pool, rather than plunging into water that is over my head?

These days, it appears that many American religious leaders will do just about anything to avoid the depths of human difficulty. There is another spirit in the air, a spirit of superficial piety and vacuous optimism. It seems to parallel the economic advancement of those who preach it.

Witness the recurring example of those who hire lights and cameras to amplify their so-called message. Listen to what they are really saying beneath the makeup and the high-priced haircuts: "You can be successful. God wants you to be rich. You were created to hoard God's abundance," and so on and so forth. There is not a calorie of nutrition in their sermons. When life hammers you with pain, they offer no real help.

Recently I sat on an ecumenical panel that was assigned to disperse grants for needy ministers. One pastor asked for funding for a sabbatical he wanted to take with his wife, particularly because the stresses of ministry were cutting into the time they could spend together. That seemed reasonable enough, and then his application revealed that his position came with a complimentary executive jet, a few big cars, and pilots and drivers to take him around. He was concerned about his share of God's work, because the demands were tugging him in so many directions. So he had requested sabbatical funds in order to study his situation and to write up some helpful publications for other pastors who were (his exact quote) "in success-based ministries."

In the name of the Jesus who thirsted and died on a cross, the panel voted down the proposal. It was a bit "too victorious" to be realistic.

I do not wish to be cruel, simply true to the scriptures and human experience. The poet who gave us Psalm 130 had spent time in the depths. The words testify to God from the bottom of the hole. And they can also testify as to how the psalmist may have ended up there.

In the Hebrew Bible, there are four different words to describe what can go wrong in our life with God. The first is transgression (*pasa*), which has to do with an act of rebellion. Somebody is in authority of your life, and you do something to declare, "No, I'm not going to go along with that." A second word is sin, from the Hebrew word *hata*, which has to do with missing a target. You aim for something, but you swerve off course. Deceit is the third Hebrew word (*remiyah*). This is a bad trait of character: unreliable, treacherous, and not to be counted upon.

The fourth word is the one that appears twice in Psalm 130. It is the Hebrew word *awon*, translated as iniquity. *Awon* describes something or someone who is bent over, twisted, or crooked.[33] Iniquity is the condition of being bent out of shape. Once all was straight, but now it is distorted. Think of a metal clothes hanger, twisted so that it no longer holds a shirt without dropping it. It cannot function as it was made to function. It has been twisted so it cannot be any good to anybody.

This is our human condition, bent and twisted. This is not the way things are supposed to be — but along the long pilgrim road, there are distortions.

Maybe you saw that item in the recent news. A man in Washington DC paid his premiums for a life insurance policy through his company. After he died, the sole beneficiary was his wife and she could not collect on it. Apparently the company

33 James Limburg, *Psalms* (Louisville, KY: Westminster John Knox Press, 2000).

switched insurers after he was diagnosed with a rare form of heart cancer and on sick leave. The new policy did not take effect until he worked one full day. His company never informed him of this requirement, which he could have done if only he knew. But he wasn't feeling well, so he stayed home, and then he died. She sued the insurance company for the money, but the suit was thrown out of court due to a loophole in the law.[34]

Theologically speaking, this is a good example of an iniquity — a situation that is not the way it is supposed to be. Something has been twisted out of shape. And this is what God is working to fix, says the psalmist. 'It is the Lord of Israel who is working to redeem all of our iniquities' …all of our short-sighted distortions …all of the hurts and harms that gnarl us into something less than human. God is always about the work of salvage and repair. Rather than keep a clipboard full of grievances against us, God is a redeemer who works to mold our lives back into their originally intended shape. God will forgive more than the rebellious transgression, the wayward sin, or the selfish lie. God is taking the whole world in for repairs.

We can admire God for that, even revere him, for this is not always our way. Left up to us, we mortals love to keep score of where we stand against all others. If possible, we would like to bump ourselves up a few notches. And in that light, we are exposed once again.

Our local funeral director pulled me aside at a recent viewing in his establishment. He said, "Watch this," and nodded toward two daughters of a woman who died. Each one was at an opposing side of the room. They would not speak to one another. They refused to look at one another. The funeral director wanted to close the casket and lead us to the cemetery, but neither daughter would leave the room as long as the other one was still there.

34 http://biz.yahoo.com/ap/080705/benefit_battles.html

Out Of The Depths

Each wanted to be the last one to say goodbye to her mother. We were there for 45 minutes waiting for one of them to finally make a move.

Beneath his breath, the funeral director muttered, "This game is called 'I Loved Mom More Than You Did.' I would bet they have been playing it since junior high school." Watching them dance around one another was to observe yet one more way to skip stones off the surface of the ocean and avoid the depths of real reconciliation.

God wants to heal our deep hurts, for God is working to save the whole world. But like every act of God, it is going to take a while. We can look toward the cross and hear Jesus pray for God's forgiveness, but people are still murdered senselessly, just like Jesus. If we trust that God answers Christ's prayer for forgiveness, as many of us do, it is still going to take a while to undo what we have done.

There will be no quick fix for global warming. No immediate relief for world hunger. No instant reconciliation of that enormous and growing gap between the global rich and poor. No quick scrubbing up of a national reputation for war-mongering. Meanwhile there are lots of sisters and other family members who still refuse to talk to one another. Biblically speaking, there are plenty of iniquities for God to redeem. Or to put it another way, millions of clothes hangers twisted out of shape. To save us beyond a quick fix, God is going to have to stay busy for an awfully long time.

The psalmist digs in for the long haul. "I wait for the Lord," he prays. "My soul waits, and in his word I hope." Then for emphasis he says it a third time, "My soul waits for the Lord, more than those who watch for the morning, more than those who watch for the morning." We wait for God to make things right. And if there is one prayer God always answers, it is the prayer to make us more patient.

As the Hebrew poetry of the psalm works on us, we find ourselves with some time on our hands. As God repairs the world, maybe we can do our part to join that work, wherever we are, in spite of whatever messes we create or find. Maybe as we come to the Lord's table, there is something we can do to join with God's work. Maybe there is a word of peace to speak, a bridge to build, a cup of cold water to share, a kindness to make tangible. Maybe we know of a child to feed, an enemy to forgive, a friend to track down. There must be something that each one of us can do.

This is how we wait for God, watch for God, hope in God. Since we have some time left on the pilgrim road, we do some of God's work *for* him. Or is it that we would do God's work *with* him? Or could it be that a patient God might be working *in us*?

Out Of The Depths

Reflection Questions

"Out Of The Depths," Psalm 130

— What are some of the difficulties of daily life that I have handled superficially?

— When have I sped past somebody in pain?

— The four Hebrew words offer a diagnosis for what's wrong with the human race: rebellion, sin, deceit, and iniquity. Which one best describes the last bad situation that I observed?

— Can I describe how something has been "bent out of shape" in my life?

— When was the last time when I sensed that God had forgiven something, either that I had done or somebody else had done?

— "Salvation" comes from the same word as "salvage." Where have I seen that God is "salvaging" the world and the people within it?

In Mother's Arms

A Song Of Ascents Of David

O LORD, my heart is not lifted up, my eyes are not raised too
high;
I do not occupy myself with things too great and too marvelous for
me.
But I have calmed and quieted my soul, like a weaned child with its
mother;
my soul is like the weaned child that is with me.
O Israel, hope in the LORD from this time on and forevermore.

(Psalm 131: 1-3)

There is a truth along the pilgrim road that nobody tells the spiritual rookie: it is possible to become cynical. If you stay at anything long enough, you might grow spiritually weary. But worse than that, you might become jaded. You can lose sight of the forest by bumping into the trees. The first bursts of enthusiasm are tempered by the realities of family and congregation.

It does not begin that way. The children might first discover the love of Jesus and then realize that mom and dad are not as excited as they are. At the end of a soul-stirring week of a youth work camp, the teenager is met by an impatient parent who holds the car keys. "Hurry up, get your things, it's time to go." A new member joins a congregation with enthusiasm but soon is gnawed upon by a few of the old crows. Somebody comes upon a season of revival, starts praying and reading the Bible, only to discover that the Bible is a very thick book and answers to prayer are not automatic. This even happens with the brand new minister, fresh from seminary, who goes out to serve a *real* church; you know, one of the old-fashioned kind of churches with the sinners still

112

inside it.

I recall the two codgers in my first church that everybody else avoided. They were universally regarded as cranky and contentious as Statler and Waldorf, the two critics who used to sit in the balcony on *The Muppet Show* and negatively comment on everything. These two parked themselves in the back corner of the sanctuary, right by the stained glass window of Jesus praying while his disciples fell asleep. That should have tipped me off.

But I was their pastor, so I thought I could befriend them. I talked about bird-watching with Statler, for that was his passion. Then I met Waldorf for dinner and he took me to see his father in the nursing home. All seemed fine until the next congregational meeting when, for whatever reason, both of them spoke out vehemently against giving me a salary increase. "Nothing personal," they said, "but the church budget is too high." The treasurer said, "But the pledges are in and the budget is balanced."

That did not matter, they shouted back. They did not think we should be spending so much money. One veteran moaned, "There they go again." They kept at it for a while. People sat and took their whipping, because that was what they were used to receiving. It was not much fun to watch and I returned home to wonder if I was serving the right church.

As we live the Christian life, there are so many things that can temper our excitement. Sometimes we are frustrated with the people around us. Other times, we are disappointed with ourselves and our own apparent lack of spiritual progress. The brief confession of Psalm 131 comes from a frustrated pilgrim. She has been at the journey for a while. In a psalm that may have been written late at night, the pilgrim surveys her soul and reports what she sees.

"O Lord, my heart is not lifted up." The destination, as we have heard, is Jerusalem, and all that it symbolizes. The journey is toward the temple, the festival, the celebration, the holy reunion. On the face of it, it is a noble pursuit. Yet here is the confession of somebody who knows of the detail and the hassles of travel. There are donkeys to be packed, lodging to be found, meals to be procured, and children to be consoled. Anybody on the road knows that travel is not an uplifting experience. A pilgrimage is both a holy journey and a pain in the neck.

If you and I had the opportunity, we could circle up our chairs and complain about the trips we have taken. Choose your topic: the price of fuel, cancelled reservations, charges for baggage, indifferent ticket agents, unusual food, phones that do not work, filthy accommodations, to say nothing of all those other obnoxious tourists. It is enough to make you think twice about ever leaving home. The heart is not lifted up by the details of travel.

And the psalmist adds, "My eyes are not raised too high." Not only are so many travel details mundane, but the excursion is not always a lofty occasion. If you journey to Bethlehem to see the birthplace of Jesus, you have to wade through the trinket sellers in Manger Square. As you approach the ruins of Corinth, the ancient city where the apostle Paul preached the gospel, the irreverent guide will mention it was a sailor's town with brothels going all the way up the hill. What were you expecting — heaven on earth? There are so few glimpses of heaven, I'm afraid, and just a lot of earth.

During a pilgrimage to the holy land, my father and I had the rare opportunity to travel to Nablus, a community in the West Bank. We were so excited about what we would see! Nablus is the location for the well of Jacob, the actual well from the fourth chapter of John where Jesus spoke to a Samaritan woman. The tour bus parked on a street full of broken glass. We traipsed through an unfinished chapel, long interrupted by Palestinian-

In Mother's Arms

Israeli skirmishes. Then we descended an uneven staircase through layers of accumulated gold and beeswax.

Circling the well, each in our group took a sip of fresh water as a New Testament professor retold the story and drew out some insights. Just then, as we were beginning to imagine the Lord speaking at this well, a surly priest interrupted and said, "Enough of that, move along, another group is right behind you. Buy your postcards and candles over here." Believe me when I say my eyes were not raised too high.

Then the psalmist says, "I do not occupy myself with things too great and too marvelous for me." How did she know? How did she know that so many Christians expect to be brought into the presence of something great and marvelous and then what they discover is the same jumbled mess of humanity that exists everywhere else?

A man was telling me about his disappointment with his church. They had a wonderful preacher and they paid him well — extremely well. In addition to his hefty salary, he had a $90,000 annual expense account, designated just for taking people out to dinner, with free prep school tuition for his children, among other benefits. There were a few rumors in the air about him, but they were dismissed as jealousy. Nobody paid much attention because whenever he preached, it was great and marvelous. Everybody was so impressed with the wonderful show.

Then one of his girlfriends posted his emails and text messages to her on a blog. His third wife got a little hot about it and left him rather publicly. Someone announced the minister had exhibited the same behavior at the other end of the state. Three prominent church leaders huddled together and agreed to pay him a half million dollars if he would slip away quietly. When his denomination got wind of this sorry business, they moved quickly to press charges — but the reverend up and quit

The Pilgrim Road

his membership and renounced their jurisdiction so that nobody could touch him. Nobody, that is, except God.

That church leader told me this story with tears in his eyes. He said, "I will never go back to that church ever again. I cannot believe what he did. I do not believe he got away with it." He was shocked and dismayed to discover the Christian church has sinners in its pulpits and pews. He no longer occupies himself with things too great and too marvelous for himself.

All who spend enough time on the pilgrim road will be tempted to lower their eyes, to reduce their expectations, and to settle for what is trivial and ugly. There is something about the holiness of God that brings out the worst in people. The immense grace of God will expose the pettiness of the church. What's the result? The faithful stop looking so high and settle for something far less than God.

There are hundreds of distractions from the spiritual journey. People will take all kinds of emotional detours that lead to dead ends. In my years as a pastor, I have known people to depart from a church over the color of the sanctuary paint, the choice to provide hospitality to a group of outsiders, the selection of elementary school curriculum, and the use of Folgers crystals during coffee hour. It is not that they switched congregations so they could get upset about something else somewhere else. What is troubling is that they simply stopped going anywhere at all — because of paint, strangers, curriculum, and instant coffee.

Just the other day, a friend told me why a family stopped attending her church. Are you ready for this? The pastor noticed the family had been absent, so he phoned to say he missed them. They were so offended by his attention that they decided to stay away — which they were already doing.

I can understand the psalmist's confession, can't you? "O Lord, my heart is not lifted up, my eyes are not raised too high;

In Mother's Arms

I do not occupy myself with things too great and too marvelous for me." Depending on how you read it, it may sound like self-disgust. Some scholars say the nuance is actually one of humility, that the psalmist admits, "I am really small-minded, O God. Save me from my pettiness."

We do not know the circumstances. As with many of the psalms, the splinters of particularity have been sanded away. What we do have is the middle verse: "I have calmed and quieted my soul like a weaned child with its mother." It points us to one of the ultimate benefits of faith, namely consolation. We may hold the heartfelt knowledge that, even if there are cranky and cynical Christians all around you, at the heart of our faith is some real help. Forgiveness can really happen. Truth can be told. Grace will cover our imperfections. Our imagination can be lifted out of the mud. God will give us quiet and calm.

This psalm sounds like it was written by a woman. I imagine her gazing down upon the nursing child on her chest. It prompts her to remember that faith provides the basic food of life. We are fed by hope, specifically the hope that the Lord of Israel is greater than all of our pettiness and short-sightedness. The very one who brought Israel out of slavery in Egypt will not allow us to be captive to our fears. "Like the child who is upon me," she says, 'so is my soul calmed by the Lord.'

One scholar suggests this poem is a lullaby, a mother's song for a whimpering infant.[35] How appropriate! "Don't let the small stuff upset you," she prays. "Lean down and rest upon your mother." That is the call to consolation — to settle down and trust God. Let go of trouble, and fall asleep. Some of us can remember the experience, even if our mothers have been gone for a while.

In many ways, the psalm resembles another famous lullaby of the scriptures, the verse that somebody called the "now I lay

35 H. Stephen Shoemaker, "Psalm 131," *Review and Expositor*, Vol. 85 (1988), 89-94.

me down to sleep" prayer of the ancient Jewish child. It comes from another psalm, Psalm 31:5, and you may remember the words: "Into your hands, I commend my spirit." Jesus quoted those words while he was on the cross.[36] Then he went to sleep, confident that all were in his parent's care.

When we are tempted to count our troubles late at night, where do we get the consolation that allows us to fall sleep? When critiques and complaints threaten to drag us down, where do we really put our trust? The psalm says, "Cuddle in close to your mother. Don't worry. Stop fretting. Be still." We never outrun this message.

I began my seminary training many years ago, but I still remember my enthusiasm. It was exciting to study and learn about Christian faith. It was not long before I realized that we had a few professors who did not care very much for congregational life. It was disturbing as a child of the church. I did not know if they had been pastors who had burned-out after a few years and went back to get their PhDs, or if they simply were teaching the wrong students in the wrong school. What I vividly remember is how they ridiculed the ministers who stuck it out, poked fun at potluck suppers, mocked the mimeograph machines, and put down anything that displayed the church with all its warts.

In my second year of study, however, a new Old Testament professor joined our faculty. Word quickly spread that he worshiped every week at one of the churches in town. Not only that, the word quickly spread how he volunteered to teach the junior high Sunday school class. Dr. Miller was not the typical professor. He had survived the teenagers and told us about his adventures in leading them through the Bible.

"It makes me a better teacher," he said. "When I teach those kids the Bible, I learn the whole thing all over again. When I tell

36 Luke 23:46.

them about the promises of God, it begins to sink in that those same promises are also for me." This is his consolation, the "pure milk" as one early Christian writer called it. To quote a few words from the first letter of Peter, "Like newborn infants, long for the pure, spiritual milk, so that by it you may grow into salvation — if indeed you have tasted that the Lord is good."[37]

The pilgrim road is long and hard enough to invite cynicism. With the psalmist we might confess, "My heart is not lifted up. My eyes are not raised too high. I am preoccupied with things that are not as great and marvelous as God." Go ahead — confess these things when you must, confess them so that you are free of them. We must never let our complaints enslave us.

And after you get them off your chest, cuddle down and offer these words from a hymn as your prayer:

"O make me thine forever, and should I fainting be,
Lord, let me never, never outlive my love to thee."[38]

37 1 Peter 2:2-3
38 "O Sacred Head, Now Wounded," stanza three — in the public domain

Reflection Questions

"In Mother's Arms," Psalm 131

— When have I been discouraged as I seek to live out my faith?

— What are some of the horror stories I can tell of faith gone bad?

— Are there ways that I have resisted the comfort of God?

— How is God like the nursing mother of this psalm?

— If I "lifted up" my eyes, what would I actually see — or not see?

— How easy is it for me to live out the Christian life over the long haul?

Finding A Home For God
A Song Of Ascents

O LORD, remember in David's favor all the hardships he endured;
how he swore to the LORD and vowed to the Mighty One of Jacob,
"I will not enter my house or get into my bed;
I will not give sleep to my eyes or slumber to my eyelids,
until I find a place for the LORD, a dwelling place for the mighty
one of Jacob."
We heard of it in Ephrathah; we found it in the fields of Jaar.
"Let us go to his dwelling place; let us worship at his footstool."
Rise up, O LORD, and go to your resting place, you and the ark of
your might.
Let your priests be clothed with righteousness, and let your faithful
shout for joy.
For your servant David's sake do not turn away the face of your
anointed one.
The LORD swore to David a sure oath from which he will not turn
back:
"One of the sons of your body I will set on your throne.
If your sons keep my covenant and my decrees that I shall teach
them,
their sons also, forevermore, shall sit on your throne."
For the LORD has chosen Zion; he has desired it for his habitation:
"This is my resting place forever; here I will reside, for I have
desired it.
I will abundantly bless its provisions; I will satisfy its poor with
bread.
Its priests I will clothe with salvation, and its faithful will shout
for joy.

The Pilgrim Road

*There I will cause a horn to sprout up for David; I have prepared a
lamp for my anointed one.*
*His enemies I will clothe with disgrace, but on him, his crown will
gleam."* (Psalm 132: 1-18)

Many of us have stories of an old-fashioned family trip. I
certainly remember a few. My father would arrive from work,
roaring up the driveway as he loosened his necktie. The car was
already packed and the snacks were in the cooler. As Dad would
run upstairs to change out of his suit, Mom would tell all of us
kids to pile into the paneled station wagon. Mom would check
that we were buckled in and then instruct us to not pinch one
another, poke one another, or cross the invisible lines on the seat
that divided us. Dad returned, ready to roll, and we went roaring
down the highway.

These were the days before iPods and Walkmans, when it was
impossible to tune out fellow passengers. So we sang songs like
"Over the River and Through the Woods," or "Oops, There Goes
Another Rubber Tree Plant," or "Little Bunny Foo-Foo."

After an hour or so, we were ready for the long trip to be over.
But not my Dad — for him, the journey had only begun. He had
the bad habit of pulling the car off the road with no warning and
rolling to a stop. Then he would hop out and read a historical
marker along the road. You know the type: "On this spot in 1779,
General John Sullivan burned an Indian village to the ground."
Or the little sign that announced how a town by the name of
Horseheads got its name.

"That was interesting," Dad announced as he returned to
the car. Putting the vehicle in gear, he would ease back onto the
highway and tell us what he read. Most of the time, the kids did
not care very much. That was history and we were in a hurry. We
often made a six-hour trip to see our grandparents. One afternoon

it struck me that it was actually a five-hour trip with a half-dozen historical markers along the way. Sometimes he stopped at a historical sign that he had visited before and we accused him of having a feeble memory. Actually he probably needed an hourly reason to escape the car from the rest of us.

The great truth is that Dad was quite interested to discover who had traveled the road before us and what had happened to them along the way. The longer I travel the pilgrim road, the more I realize that such curiosity is a rare and important gift.

All of us have our own historical markers. A couple exchanges wedding vows by an oak tree, at the place where they first kissed. The family reunion circles around the old homestead, where so many of their lives began. The elementary school was always a home away from home, even if now the ceilings seem so small. Even a favorite church can seem like holy geography. As the reformers reminded us, a sanctuary is only a room. It cannot contain God. Yet God promises to meet us here as we meet one another. Mark the site: "On this spot, something happened."

That we should mark such a place for all future generations is instructive. A lot of Christians do not have any interest in what happened before they were born. It is part of the self-indulgence of our times to think that faith begins and ends with us. We mislead ourselves in thinking we are the first believers to make the pilgrim journey that our struggles and delights are the only ones that matter, or that nothing of significance ever happened to anybody else along this particular highway. Some of us have been heard to grumble that paying attention to history only slows down the trip.

But the road of faith is filled with historical markers. On that spot in 1000 BC, something happened. In this city in 587 BC, invaders broke through the city wall, demolished our holy places, and took away our brightest and best. On this hill in 30

AD, somebody who loved us was crucified and killed. In that graveyard three days later, his corpse came alive and broke out of the tomb. We cannot believe unless we remember.

In Psalm 132, this is what the psalmist did along the pilgrim road. He was moving toward Jerusalem and he remembered. Specifically, he recalled King David, the greatest of all Israel's kings.

One day, went the story, David was resting from battle. As he looked around his palace, he said, "This is a wonderful home, but something is not right. I am living in a house of the finest cedar, but the ark of God stays merely in a tent. God needs a proper house." The prophet Nathan nodded in agreement and said, "You know what you must do."

But that night, the Lord God crept into one of Nathan's dreams. "Go and tell David that I don't live in a house," said the Lord. "I have traveled with a tent, and I have spoken from a tent. I have no need for real estate. So go and remind my servant David that I found him in a sheep pasture. I have traveled with him as he wandered, and kept him safe from every threat. The time will come when I will plant my people in a chosen place, and give them rest from their enemies."

Then the Lord said, "Go and tell my David, if anybody plans to build a house, it's going to be me. I will build an eternal house for David, a perpetual house of his offspring, established forever."[39]

Listen: this was one of the great promises of God. From David, a child would come who will rule forever and ever. The Savior of Israel will establish the house of David and all that it symbolizes and stands for. That is the hope for a Messiah.

Meanwhile, after King David died, one of his sons built a house for God anyway. Solomon built the most magnificent temple, a permanent home for the God who was accustomed

39 The story is told in 2 Samuel 7:1-13.

to traveling in a tent. It was a place to honor the Creator who made the earth and filled it with rich blessings, to worship the redeemer who freed the faithful from their various slaveries, and to welcome the Spirit who teaches all who walk in the holy paths of love and righteousness. These are the reasons to build God a house: thanksgiving, worship, and instruction. This is why people still build each sanctified structure. They seek a place to encounter God.

That does not mean that, even if we build the house ourselves, we can be certain that God will be home. The one who is Creator, redeemer, and Spirit does not always seem to remain indoors.

The old crook Jacob found that out the hard way. He stole the family blessing from his twin brother Esau and then he ran off into the wilds. Jacob was pretty sure that Esau was right behind him, carrying a blunt instrument, so he ran as fast as he could. When night fell, and he was too tired to go any further, he laid down to sleep on a big rock — and he dreamed of angels! They were coming down with the blessings of heaven, and climbing back up with the needs of earth. The vision startled him awake. What did he exclaim? "Truly the Lord is in this place, and I did not know it!" It was good news, but it was terrifying news. He had been found — is there anybody who really wants to be found? Yes — and no. In the midst of all his deceptions, there was a God beyond himself who saw the truth. That is dangerous. Yet this God did not strike him down. That is the essence of grace.

So Jacob took some oil and anointed that stone pillow of his. He left behind a historical marker, calling the place "Beth-El," which means "the house of God." (Genesis 28:10-17)

God can show up anywhere, as God is free to come and go. This is both the promise and predicament for pilgrims. Nobody outruns God, and yet God can keep distant or God can come, ready or not.

The Pilgrim Road

That is what the church believes about Jesus, too. Death could not hold him, so the risen Lord is free to come and go. Even before that, he told a couple of followers, "You will see heaven opened, and the angels of God ascending and descending upon the Son of Man."[40] To put it another way, Jesus is Beth-El, the "house of God," the one in whom humanity meets divinity. He "pitched his tent and lived among us," said the gospel of John,[41] for heaven could not hold Jesus any more than the grave did.

Some looked at Jesus and saw God's glory and others looked and saw nothing special. Some looked at him and heard God's promise to David, "One of the sons of your body I will set on your throne." Others were not so sure. This is how faith reveals and conceals. If you look and see or believe that you have seen, what you see can change you.

Once, as I traveled in a Greek tour bus from Thessaloniki to Philippi, our guide pointed to a foggy shape along the Aegean Sea. "There, you can see Mount Athos," Loula said. The Holy Mountain, as it is known, is the Vatican City of the Orthodox Church. It is closed off from the rest of the world, available to a mere handful of visitors, many of whom are turned away. Since the sixth century AD, hundreds of monks have lived in some twenty monasteries and a number of caves. They have spent their entire adult lives in worship, reflection, and prayer.

"Loula," I said, "what can you tell me about the people who go to Mount Athos?"

She stared intently and said, "If they ever return at all, they are changed. On the Holy Mountain of Athos, people have seen God."

Or to put it another way, "On this spot something happened."

As we travel the pilgrim road, what we want is an encounter

40 John 1:51
41 John 1:14 (Literal Translation).

with God. What we fear is an encounter with God. It has always been that way. Spiritual experience is both compelling and repelling. We have heard it before: we fear God because we love God. A place of worship is where God can meet us.

The psalmist knew this. That is one of the reasons why we have Psalm 132. It offers a historical marker for the Jerusalem temple. This was the house David wanted to build to worship the Lord, and this was the footstool where a heavenly God touched down on earth. This was where the priests got dressed up for their liturgies and the faithful "raise the roof" in song. For whatever reason, this was the place God chose for his habitation, sang the psalmist.

But when the psalmist prayed, he asked that the Lord God almighty might actually show up. In the central petition of the prayer, he said, "Rise up, O Lord, and go to your resting place, you and the ark of your might." We can pray for God's presence, but it is not automatic. Maybe that's a good thing. If the living God was to come, who could stand? All sin would be exposed, all injustice would be obvious, all superficiality would be burned away, and in their place would shine the glory of God, and we would be changed.

One summer, my wife and I spent some time on an island in Scotland. It is a bleak and desolate place, with fields of peat as far as the eye can see. On Sunday morning an austere congregation welcomed us in their barren sanctuary. As is their custom, we sang five psalms without accompaniment and listened to a long sermon in Gaelic. At 6:00 that evening, we returned to do it all over again, this time in English, with five different psalms, and a different sermon. Believe me when I tell you, there was not much else to do on the sabbath in that town.

The wind whistled outside as the preacher thundered in his pulpit. Through the window, I saw a few sea birds flying sideways. It was hard to tell how they could possibly remain in the air.

Then we got in the car and drove the long way back to town. It was a beautiful night, so we decided to chase after the sunset. Across the moors we drove, along patches of heather, sometimes encouraged by herds of indifferent sheep. It wasn't long before we came upon a group of standing stones. The Callanish Stones are huge five-ton monoliths, about thirty in all. An ancient tribe carried them to that spot and stuck them in the ground. They have been standing in the shape of a Celtic cross for five thousand years. They were magnificent and mysterious, back-dropped by what had become a purple and orange sherbet-colored sky. Anthropologists can only suggest why those stones are there, but one thing is clear: this was an ancient worship sanctuary.

The contrast couldn't have been more striking: an austere church with ten psalms and two sermons, an ancient stone shrine predating both Christians and Jews with a near-deafening wind as its only sound. On each spot, I wanted to leave a marker that said, "Something happened here." Each in its own right was beautiful and awe-filled. Neither location could contain the fullness of God, but each pointed to it. Indoors, we sang of God's covenantal love. Outdoors, there was fierce, holy indifference. In these two bleak temples, God was both available and absent at the same time, close at hand, yet maddeningly elusive. The experience was as terrifying as it was inviting. My heart was strangely warmed, but my eyebrows felt slightly singed. I did not have much to say for the next forty minutes as we returned through the howling moors.

"On this spot, something happened." The tourists speed by in a hurry, never pausing to read the signs, but the pilgrim prepares for the deeper experience. God can meet us anywhere, in the howling wind or the humming psalm, within whitewashed walls or among granite stones. The elusive creator, the risen Christ, the wind of God's Spirit — the Triune God can come, actually come. We simply never know how or where, so we have to stay open. We remember God came among us. We pray for it to happen again.

In the mid-1970s, the priest Henri Nouwen spent seven months in a Trappist monastery near Rochester, New York. As he participated in the patterns of this very organized religious institution — the liturgy, the silence, the regulated rhythms of the day and week — he gradually understood that, at its best, the structure was not for itself but, rather, to "create space for God." He wrote in his journal, "The monk, more than anyone else, realizes that God dwells only where we step back to give him room."[42]

He went on to say, "Monks go to a monastery to find God. But monks who live in a monastery as if they had found God are not real monks... God should be sought, but we cannot find God. We can only be found by him."[43]

Along the pilgrim road, the sun threatens to strike by day and the moon by night. There are enemies on each side and demons that tempt from within. We travel one day with burdensome luggage and the next with a sack full of thank-you notes. Yet as pilgrims, we never lose sight of the journey's purpose: to make ourselves available to God. We pay attention to the places where God has gone before and we go where God might find us.

Should that happen, let us agree in advance that we will do our best to stay found.

42 Henri J. M. Nouwen, *The Genesee Diary: Report From A Trappist Monastery* (Garden City, New York: Doubleday, 1976), 148.
43 Henri Nouwen, *The Genessee Diary*, 118..

Reflection Questions

"Finding A Home For God," Psalm 132

— Is there a special place where I have encountered the presence of God?

— If God can go anywhere, why do I meet God in specific places?

— How do I mark my memories?

— Where are some of the pilgrimages that I have made to extraordinary places?

— Did the sites live up to their promise?

— Where are the places that I go for sustenance, restoration, and renewed vision?

— What can I do to protect those places and keep them special?

Kindred Companions
A Song Of Ascents

How very good and pleasant it is when kindred live together in
unity!
It is like the precious oil on the head,
running down upon the beard, on the beard of Aaron,
running down over the collar of his robes.
It is like the dew of Hermon, which falls on the mountains of Zion.
For there the LORD ordained his blessing, life forevermore.
(Psalm 133: 1-3)

How good it is. "How very good and pleasant it is when kindred live together in unity!" Once in a while, it is comforting to have a Bible passage that you immediately understand. There are not a lot of difficult words to look up in the dictionary. No mind-numbing theological concepts to pin down. This psalm simply proclaims that it is a beautiful thing when people get along and live in peaceful community.

That is the theme of Psalm 133. Two ancient illustrations are given to tickle the senses. When people live in peace, what is it like? It is like the oil of an abundant blessing, spilling all over your cheeks and dribbling into your beard. Those with beards can understand the analogy, while the rest of us can only imagine. As Lawrence Cunningham notes,

> *There are lines that have never made sense to me but which have*
> *an unforgettable poetic power. Why, for instance, is the unity of*
> *brethren "like the precious oil upon the head, running down on the*
> *collar" (Psalm 133)? I do not know, but I do know that few lines*
> *are more beautiful than that praise of fraternal community.*[44]

44 Lawrence Cunningham, "Praying the Psalms," *Theology Today* (April 1989, volume 46, number 1) 43.

The Pilgrim Road

What is it like? How shall we describe it when everybody gets along? It is like the morning dew falling on the mountains, watering the thirsty soil, and dribbling down to fill the stream. We did not ask for the dew. It fell from heaven like a gift — just like the oil of that blessing. And that is how it feels to find that there are people in your life who have been given to you as a gift.

This is the heart of what the psalmist sang in this brief poem. It does not matter if we translate the first verse literally. In Hebrew the text sounds like a fraternity house, as in "How pleasing is the dwelling of brothers together." Or we can generalize and expand it, as Stephen Mitchell translated the same thought: "How wonderful it is to live in harmony with all people."[45] Either way the meaning is clear: it is a holy gift to have companions as we travel the pilgrim road. It is a blessing from God to have people who share our life. It is good and pleasant to have sisters, brothers, and friends living together in peace. How good this is!

For the next few minutes, I want you to think of a face. When you think of good and pleasant company, who is the first person that comes to mind? Can you see a face? While you mull that over, let me share how writer Frederick Buechner described his first real friend:

Like me, he was kind of oddball — plump and not very tall then with braces on his teeth and glasses that kept slipping down the short bridge of his nose and a rather sarcastic, sophisticated way of speaking that tended to put people off — and for that reason, as well as for the reason that he was a good deal brighter than most of us, including me, boys tended to make his life miserable. But it was Jimmy who became my first great friend, and it was through coming to know him that I discovered that perhaps I was not, as I had always suspected, alone in the universe and the only one of my kind. He was another who saw the world enough as I saw it

45 Stephen Mitchell, A Book of Psalms: Selected and Adapted from the Hebrew (New York: HarperCollins, Publishers, 1993) 73.

*to make me believe that maybe it was the way the world actually
was.*[46]

How good it is to have a friend like that — somebody who
sees the same world you see. Can you see a face? Can you see the
face of some kindred soul?

Sometimes we discover them out of shared interests or
experience. We may not have chosen these people, but suddenly
we discover they are with us. C.S. Lewis said friendship happens
when two or more people discover they have something in
common. Up until that point, each of them believes she or he is
alone, bearing some unique treasure or burden. Then comes the
discovery, said Lewis, and friendship begins when one of them
says, "What? You too? I thought I was the only one."[47]

How good it is to discover you are not alone, that you are
never *alone*. Even if you talk to yourself and live by yourself,
you are always part of a larger company. Surely that is what
the psalmist was singing about. The pilgrim had been moving
gradually toward Jerusalem for worship. In this next-to-last Song
of Ascents, she paused to celebrate that there are others on the
same journey.

We know how it is. Say we are on an airplane, or riding a
bus, or driving down a crowded highway. It is possible to be
surrounded by other travelers and still think we are the only ones
taking the trip. We isolate ourselves without acknowledging we
have done so. Maybe we are so focused on the destination that
we have stopped paying attention to those on parallel journeys.
Or we are jamming to the music on earbuds, insolated from all
conversation. Suddenly this wide-awake traveler wakes up to
realize, "I do not have to be alone. God has enlarged my little

46 Frederick Buechner, The Sacred Journey (New York: HarperCollins Publishers, 1982)
70.
47 C. S. Lewis, *The Four Loves* (New York: Harcourt Brace Jovanovich, Inc., 1960), 96.

world and put others around me, and that is a great blessing."

In Geoffrey Chaucer's *The Canterbury Tales*, he described a large company of people making a shared pilgrimage to the cathedral of Canterbury, to see some sacred bones. He surveyed the crowd and discovered everybody had a story to tell. Everybody had a tale. Everybody could speak of what had brought them this far; some stories were downright comical and bawdy, and others were virtuous and self-assured. Each pilgrim told their tale along the way, and the conversation was the best way to pass the time. There's the baker, the soldier, the miller's wife....

But beneath it all was the reality of a community. The spiritual life looks less a private voyage and more like an over-subscribed bus trip. Everybody was carrying their luggage, people were hanging on and shaking through the highway's bumps, yet all of them were moving — or being moved — to the same destination. Like many bus trips, the longer the journey, the deeper the companionship. Travelers started sharing their Cheetos across the aisle. Somebody asks if anybody would like an extra apple. One helpful soul offered a hint on the crossword puzzle that another was doing across the aisle. All the time, they were being commonly carried to the same destination.

This is not a bad snapshot of the community that surrounds us as we travel the Christian life.

About two hundred years before the New Testament was written, there was another Jewish teacher named Jesus. His name was Jesus Ben Sirach. He lived long enough to go around the block a few times. An astute and careful observer of daily life, Ben Sirach compiled many wise sayings which were later published in a book. It is a warm and practical book, even if it has not been included in most of our Bibles. Three of his sayings are descriptions of faithful friends:

Kindred Companions

- Faithful friends are a sturdy shelter: whoever finds one has found a treasure.

- Faithful friends are beyond price; no amount can balance their worth.

- Faithful friends are life-saving medicine; and those who fear the Lord will find them.[48]

This is the same message the psalmist announced. If we love God, if we honor God, if we move as lifelong pilgrims toward God, we can look around and see those people that God has appointed to join us on the journey. They will enrich our spirit and enlarge our world, and they are a blessing that may surprise us. Can you see a face? Can you think of a name?

I can think of a few. One of my fellow travelers is a woman named Virginia. As far as I can remember, we met over three decades ago. It was a meeting at a church in the western Catskill Mountains of New York. I was there to testify that I had heard God calling me toward ministry. About a hundred people sat on hard wooden pews and listened to my story. God's voice had spoken in a whisper, and I did what I could to amplify what I had heard as impressively as possible.

The church people in that room were either bemused or astonished enough to allow me to explore all of this further. But from the vantage point of decades of Christian experience, the most important moment on that day was when a thin lady in brown hair and glasses sauntered up and introduced herself. She was a couple years older than me. She was already attending the seminary to which I planned to apply. She mentioned she was serving as an intern in a church not far from where I grew up, and if I had any questions about what lay ahead, I was welcome

48 Sirach 20:14-16.

to ask. We smiled quietly at one another, stood awkwardly for another minute, and that was that.

Little did I know that God would keep putting her in my life for the next 35 years. I finished college, was accepted at the seminary, and began to study. One day at the beginning of my final year, Virginia reappeared in the seminary. Her two-year internship was over, and she was returning with the great wisdom of parish life, which she would apply to her remaining academic studies. This has continued to be a theme for our friendship. Whenever one of us reads a book or gets a half-cocked idea, the other one of us is present to yank the hot air balloon back down to earth. If the truth be told, she is usually the one yanking my chain.

We have a lot in common. Both of us are firstborn children, always assuming that others are lining up behind us. Both of us were raised by smart parents in small towns who pushed us to reach beyond our upbringings. Both of us grew up in Sunday schools and sanctuaries, and both of our families were the last to leave coffee hour in their churches. Both of us still believe that, even though congregations have the potential to drive us crazy, they really are the focal points for living out the Christian life. And we believe a "solitary Christian" is a contradiction in terms.

It is a strange and wonderful friendship that we share. There have been long gaps over the years when we did not talk much or keep in touch. We have also been seatmates in airplanes and automobiles, logging thousands of miles in travel to meetings and conferences. Sometimes we talk the whole way, other times we are mute for long stretches — either way, the miles fly by.

As with any good friendship, we have endured with one another through suffering. Virginia fought breast cancer, while I am a divorce survivor. Each has gasped at the other's pain, but neither of us ever intruded, hovered, or offered empty promises. Each of us went through the necessary therapies and emerged as healthier people. We have wept, laughed, and yelled at one another. We continue to share struggles, laugh at foibles, express anger, and even offer a corrective word. All of it happens with profound mutual respect.

At points, we have found ourselves under the authority of one another's leadership. When I have been appointed to the board of a church organization, I always wanted her wisdom and pulled strings to get her assigned to the same group. When I remarried, it was her church's organist that I wed. Naturally we asked Virginia to conduct the wedding, and I had to endure her premarital counseling and grant her creative control over my nuptials.

However, I still find ways to get even. One Sunday when I was on vacation, I sneaked into her organ loft and improvised a jazz prelude. Then I sat with a cup of coffee and tried to read a book during her sermon. Dang, if she didn't keep interrupting me with her good words!

Here is the important thing: neither of us ever expected a friendship like this. Early on, we might have voted one another "least likely to ever be my friend." She has had numerous reasons to vote me off her island, but God keeps putting us in this friendship which has grown over the course of so many years. I cannot imagine living my Christian faith without her companionship. How good it is.

"How very good and pleasant it is when kindred live together in unity!"

I know what the psalmist was singing about, don't you? Can you see a face? Can you survey your life, and name those people who were given to you as a sheer gift? Maybe they are related to you, or maybe they aren't. But God puts good companions in our lives for a while, and their presence can offer a deep blessing. They enrich us. They call our attention to matters otherwise neglected. They raise our sights toward visions too great for our imagination.

In the opening pages of John Irving's wonderful novel, *A Prayer for Owen Meany*, the narrator says,

> *I am doomed to remember a boy with a wrecked voice — not because of his voice, or because he was the smallest person I ever knew... but because he is the reason I believe in God; I am a Christian because of Owen Meany... I skip a Sunday service now and then; I make no claims to be especially pious; I have a church rummage faith — the kind that needs patching up every weekend. What faith I have I owe to Owen Meany, a boy I grew up with. It is Owen who made me a believer.*[49]

How good it is to have a kindred companion like that! Can you think of a face? Can you write down a name? Find the margin of your worship bulletin, and write down that name. Hang on to that name. No matter what happens, hold on to that name.

Sometime this week, perhaps you could send a note to that person and say, "I thank my God whenever I think of you..."

49 John Irving, *A Prayer for Owen Meany* (New York: Ballantine Books, 1990), 3.

Reflection Questions

"Kindred Companions," Psalm 133

— When I think of my friends, who is the first person who comes to mind?

— What were the circumstances of our meeting?

— How has that companionship been sustained?

— What do we share in common, and how do we differ?

— How has that friendship enlarged my heart?

— What would be lost if that friendship were lost?

— Who are the new friends that God is bringing into my life?

— How can I nurture those friendships?

Antiphonal Blessings

A Song Of Ascents

Come, bless the LORD, all you servants of the LORD,
who stand by night in the house of the LORD!
Lift up your hands to the holy place, and bless the LORD.
May the LORD, maker of heaven and earth, bless you from Zion.

(Psalm 134: 1-3)

On the day I officially became the pastor of my congregation, a good friend charged me with a few words. At one point, he held up a colorful insert from the morning paper and declared, "The comics come out on Sunday." Indeed, they do. My congregation is full of comedians. Some of them have no clue how comical they are.

You should see the faces that many of them make while I preach. Some smile pleasantly, especially when I speak of sin. Some start to frown when we wade into the deeper water of the pool. A listener might sit cross-armed in resistance, as if to say, "You're not going to get through to me." Or there is the occasional shock of recognition, as if the Holy Spirit whispers, "Hey pal, he is talking about you."

This not only happens when I preach sermons. Since I am the only person who has an official reason to keep my eyes open when I lead a prayer, it might surprise you to discover who else is peeking while we pray.

And, of course, there are countless varieties of ways that our folks greet the offering plate as it passes down each pew. Some give with enthusiasm, others wave it by, a few pretend they do not even see it.

But it is from the back of the sanctuary that I see all the comics

140

for who they really are. They are the church, the people of God. By the last verse of the final hymn, I make my way down the center aisle and set my hymnal on the edge of the last pew. Raising my hands in benediction, I pronounce a blessing upon the backs of their heads. I lift my hands, and I bless them.

This is an unusual thing to do. Each week, I see such an assortment of souls: the conscientious volunteer, the forgetful leader, the henpecked grandfather, the single mother, the teenager with secrets, the woman with a disagreeable smile. All of them may be here, and each one receives the same blessing. This is the church of Jesus Christ at its best.

A few of them throw me a sideways glance as I move down the aisle. Twenty seconds later, the organ will play departure music, and everybody will be scattered to the four winds. In that moment, however, I have them in the palm of my hand. And I reflect on what I should say.

"Go in peace to love and serve the Lord." Those are my usual words. The charge is brief and direct. It affirms both the gospel of reconciliation and the mandate of Christian service. It is a last minute reminder that life is about something more than one's own whims and habits. We go in peace to love and serve.

Then I say what everybody has waited to hear: *"The grace of the Lord Jesus Christ, the love of God, and the fellowship of the Holy Spirit be with you all, now and forever."* That was Saint Paul's benediction for the tangled church of Corinth, so I figure it is a worthy prayer for my beloved congregation. I look at the backs of their balding, wigged, or tussled heads — and I pronounce the blessing of God upon them.

This is one of the rare privileges of my calling. I give the benediction — the word literally in Latin means to speak "a good word." And I quietly pray the blessing will last beyond the parking lot.

The Pilgrim Road

In Psalm 134, the last of the songs of ascent, the pilgrims end their journey with a blessing. Three times, they speak the Hebrew verb *barak* — the good word that means "blessing." Each of the three sentences offers a verb of invitation: "Bless the Lord," "Lift your hands and bless the Lord," "May the Lord bless you."

Maybe this was the psalmist's intention. We have prayed fifteen psalms along the pilgrim road. The trip began with discomfort in a foreign land. The road was steep and hard. The pilgrim was scorned by those on an easier path. Along the way we remember the challenges, the weariness, the enemies and friends. We work through the troubles around us and the resistance within our hearts. When we finally arrive, there is a blessing. We have awaited and expected the good word, the final word: "God bless you!"

But this is actually the second half of the blessing. Twice we are called upon to "bless the Lord." Not only is it God's blessing to shower us with the gifts of well-being, the psalm invites us to put aside all our complaints and say a good word about God. The Bible talks about God before it talks about us, and that is pretty much the pattern for how blessings are supposed to work.

Many times, the Bible calls on us to "bless the Lord." Perhaps the most familiar invitation is the opening verse of Psalm 103: "Bless the Lord, my soul, and all that is within me, bless God's holy name." Then the psalm says it again, "Bless the Lord, O my soul, and forget not all God's benefits...." A long list of benefits is then given: God redeems life in the pit, God forgives sins, God heals diseases, God satisfies people with good things as long as they live.

"Count your blessings," in other words. That was the psalmist's invitation. Make a list of all these benefits and it will point us toward the God who showers them upon us! God may be invisible, but God's blessings are all around us. We do not ask for all the good things we receive. We could not even begin to count them, because there are more than we can number. God is simply that generous. To "bless the Lord" is to name God's goodness as specifically as we can.

But that is easier said than done.

When Lucretia passed away, people said her difficulties were finally over. If the truth be told, she decided to merely perpetuate them. Every time anybody talked with her, she had little good to say. Her children did not turn out so well. Her husband never brought home enough money. The house was too small. Her friends did not pay enough attention to her and so on. When someone is so sour about so many things, it is a tell-tale sign of her displeasure with God.

Unfortunately, it did not stop there. After she was widowed, she moved south. Shortly after that, she became ill and died. "Bitter to the last drop," one neighbor observed. When her three children gathered at the attorney's office following the funeral, they discovered that one of them had been written out of the will. It was not done nicely. "I despise my daughter," she wrote, "and everything that she represents."

It began years ago, when Lucretia criticized her daughter Lori for spending too much time at her church. A weekly Bible study meant Lori had to change the hour she took Lucretia for groceries and she heard about it. When Lori decided to begin studying at a seminary, her mother said, "You are wasting your time." As she went through the steps to become ordained by the United Methodist Church, Lucretia said, "You would be a terrible minister; then again, I have never known a good one." When Lucretia died, she insulted Lori in her will and refused to leave her a dime. Bitter to the last drop.

The most painful detail for me is that hers was one of the heads that I blessed every Sunday morning for about fifteen years. How

143

can someone stand to receive the blessing of God, and then turn to curse those closest to her? I think it begins when people stop blessing the Lord.

To bless the Lord is to praise the Lord. When addressed to God in Hebrew prayer and song, blessing and praising are the same task. The joyful work set before every pilgrim is to praise our souls out of despair, to drown our complaints with doxologies. We sing the great hymns that set us free and this trains us to look beyond ourselves to the God in whose presence is abundant life and perfect light.

Certainly the difficulties come along the pilgrim road, we encounter them again and again. But difficulties must not define us. We belong to God. God is the alpha and omega, the beginning and end, our source and destination. God made us and did so in a way to stay hidden from us. The spiritual journey begins by waking up to how this world cannot meet our deepest needs, apart from the generosity of God. We start out, maybe out of religious routine, yet always taking steps that move us toward the presence of our benefactor. And when we arrive, fully aware of our blessing, it is due in no small part to our habit of praising and blessing God.

Yes, it must become a habit. Like any habit, praising and blessing take repeated effort. They take root in us only if we keep practicing them. A musician can fake it for only so long before lack of practice begins to show. A seamstress cannot get the stitches straight without doing a thousand of them first. The occasional gardeners will not see much of a crop unless they learn to love soil and seasons.

In the same way, we cannot bless the Lord once and believe that we are done with it. The praises must crawl into our souls. We must practice being thankful until we are grateful. We must practice saying "good words" until they re-script our lives. Most of all, we must never be content with trace amounts of the Holy Spirit in the air.

In the words of the letter to the Ephesians, "Be filled with the Spirit, as you sing psalms, hymns, and spiritual songs among yourselves, singing and making melody to the Lord in your hearts, giving thanks to God the Father at all times and for everything in the name of our Lord Jesus Christ" (Ephesians 5:18b-20).

To live this way is to live in freedom. We are free from our own achievements, free from our own failures, free from maintaining our reputations — and free to rely on the blessings of God. That is all we need, and it usually means we have a sense of humor about ourselves.

I like the story I heard about Karl Barth, perhaps the greatest Christian theologian of the twentieth century. He had a brilliant mind and a great sense of humor. Eugene Peterson tells how one day, Barth was traveling on a bus in his town, when a tourist got on and sat right beside him. Apparently, it was easy to spot him as a tourist; it usually is.

Dr. Barth struck up a conversation, asking, "Are you new to our city?" "Oh yes," said the tourist.

"What would you like to see in our city?" asked Barth. The man said, "I would like to see the great theologian Karl Barth. He is one of the world's great thinkers and writers, and I am very impressed with his work. Do you know him?"

"Do I know him? Why, I regularly give him a close shave and trim his eyebrows." The tourist was so impressed, and shook his hand. Then he got off the bus and started bragging to all who would listen that he had just met the great theologian's barber![50]

If we bless the Lord, and give all credit to the Lord, we have no need for shallow pride. Life is about the goodness of God, the

50 Eugene Peterson, *A Long Obedience in the Same Direction* (Downers Grove: InterVarsity Press, 1978), 190.

grace and justice of God, the blessings that come freely from a hand more generous than our own. We must train ourselves to see it and receive it. Then comes the truth: we are blessed that we might become a blessing to others.

This is where the journey takes us. The pilgrim road leads us to the place in our lives where we bless and enjoy God forever. It is so abundant that it will spill all over those around us. We discover anew what lies at the heart of the spiritual life: we receive the gifts of God and pass them along with holy generosity. The first and final gift is the blessing of God.

I conclude these reflections on a hilltop in southern New York. I have come to spend a few days in a monastery that doubles as a working sheep farm. The lambs bleat their flat praises as the sun slips over the hillside. Soon the chapel bell will chime, calling all pilgrims to Compline, the final prayer service of the day.

This is my favorite of the daily worship services. There is a calm that settles upon the candlelit chapel. The lengthening shadows are punctured by candlelight. A plaintive harp accompanies our singing. The final psalm of the long day is this one, Psalm 134, and the words descend upon us all. "Bless the Lord!" "Bless the Lord!" "May the Lord bless all of you!"

It is a glimpse of my final destination and yours. We have traveled as pilgrims to this moment when all is hushed and full of peace. Tomorrow will begin another day, full of surprise and challenge. There will be stress and striving, toil and snare. But for now, right now, we are bound to praise and enjoy God. This is our end. And it is a gift to rehearse it before it comes.

Antiphonal Blessings

Reflection Questions

"Antiphonal Blessings," Psalm 134

- When was the most recent time somebody blessed me with words?

- How did it change the moment?

- Can I name two dozen blessings that God has provided so far this day?

- What do these blessings teach me about God?

- Can I trust that everything in my life will turn out well?

- If I were to write a benediction on my life, what would it say?

- Would this be the same or different benediction that I would offer for others?

CPSIA information can be obtained
at www.ICGtesting.com
Printed in the USA
BVHW071203100121
597421BV00002B/108

9 780788 029585